The Century Psychology Series
Richard M. Elliott, *Editor*

DEVELOPMENT IN ADOLESCENCE

Development in Adolescence

APPROACHES TO THE STUDY OF THE INDIVIDUAL

BY

HAROLD E. JONES

ASSISTED BY

The Staff of the Adolescent Growth Study
Institute of Child Welfare
University of California

APPLETON-CENTURY-CROFTS
EDUCATIONAL DIVISION
New York MEREDITH CORPORATION

PRINTED IN THE UNITED STATES OF AMERICA
390–48649–3

TO

JOHN SANDERS

AND HIS CLASSMATES

WHOSE COÖPERATION

MADE THIS BOOK POSSIBLE

Contents

Illustrations

Tables

Preface

The principal method of studying human growth and development is through the comparison of data collected at different maturity levels. Within this method, several variations are feasible. The data to be compared may refer to the same individuals observed through time, or to different individuals sampled from groups of differing maturity. The data may refer to a single aspect of development, such as mental or motor ability, or to several aspects considered jointly. Each of these types of research material has its special value, and each has been used to supplement others in connection with various problems of development.

The present report is based on records obtained for a single person over a period of seven years. The individual in question, whom we have called John Sanders, was selected from a grade-group of eighty boys, in a growth study consisting originally of approximately 200 boys and girls.[1] It is perhaps difficult to say why "John Sanders" was chosen for this presentation, rather than any other of his classmates; others might have served the general purpose equally well, although some special interest attaches to this case because he presents, in somewhat sharpened form, a

[1] The group of which John was a member consisted of urban public school children, drawn from five elementary schools representing different social and economic areas. Two of these schools were in or near residential districts; two (including the school attended by John) were in an average middle class area, and one adjoined an industrial district. At the end of the sixth grade, these schools graduated their pupils into a single junior high school. The growth study, continuing to the end of senior high school, included an intensive program of physical and physiological measurements and records of various aspects of behavioral development during adolescence. The general plan of the study has been described in the following two references: H. E. Jones, "The California Adolescent Growth Study," *Journal of Educational Research*, Vol. 31, 1936, pp. 561-567; and H. E. Jones, "Procedures of the Adolescent Growth Study," *Journal of Consulting Psychology*, Vol. 3, 1939, pp. 177-180.

number of problems which are of common occurrence in contemporary urban culture. In the case of John, these problems of adjustment are less remarkable for severity than for variety. John has been handicapped by unhappy relationships within his family; economic stress; ill health; visual defects; an inferior physique; delayed maturity; a certain obtuseness in social contacts; lack of athletic abilities; and lack of ability to win goals which he has most desired in connection with a strong drive for popularity and social esteem. Under this heavy accumulation of handicaps his school career has been notable for a cycle of personal difficulties followed by some degree of success and effective adjustment. Viewing the record of John Sanders from the sixth grade to college, one cannot help being impressed by the amount of idiosyncrasy to be observed within a "normal" range; and by the complexity of problems which can be faced and even to some extent surmounted within a social structure that has done little to provide sympathetic support or understanding.

The research materials on which this report is based could be organized in various ways. One might, for example, use the method of biography, combining into a single view all that is known about an individual for a given period of life. In this method, trends in various characteristics are treated not by themselves but in some conceptual relation to the individual as a whole. The present report serves a different purpose and follows a different course. Its chapters deal not with successive age levels or growth stages of a total individual, but rather with specific modes of expression of a total growth process. More or less independent sections of the data are treated in such a way that a reader interested in a specific approach can observe the application of this method and study an example of individual development as portrayed by it. The concluding chapter deals primarily with interrelationships basic to construction of "the individual as a whole"; however, since any such interpretation must include a fair amount of conjecture, the reader whose interests lie in this field is for the most part left free to develop his own hypotheses.

No claim can be made for the completeness of this presentation, for we have found it necessary to exclude a large amount of recorded personal data. In this way, all references have been eliminated which would be so clearly identifying as to spoil the incognito under which the Sanders family is presented. Such processes of selection offer hazards. They can be used, consciously or unconsciously, to exclude materials which fail to fit the writer's preconceptions, thus giving a glamorous air of consistency to the documents that are retained. In the present instance, particular care has been taken to avoid such selection, through the use of criticisms based on the independent judgments of four staff members, each of whom is well acquainted with John and with the total body of records.

Until recently, our chief evidence about the adolescent period has been derived from studies which emphasize group results (for example, averages, age norms, mass correlations). This is understandable, since the testing of methods and of general hypotheses requires reliable evidence from many cases; competent investigators are not usually satisfied to work for long within the limited domain of a single case, which is properly regarded as a source of questions rather than of general conclusions. Nevertheless, as a teaching vehicle—to illustrate method and to present specific growth phenomena concretely rather than abstractly—a detailed survey of individual development may be assumed to have certain merits. Such a survey must necessarily include some reference to normative or group data, for individual characteristics can be fairly appraised only if seen in relation to individual differences. Our records of John Sanders will therefore be presented (wherever this is possible) against the perspective of the group as a whole.

The present study is one of a series of reports on the individual and the group in adolescence. It appeared originally, in preliminary form and for limited circulation, as the joint production of seven members of the staff of the Adolescent Growth Study. In the present edition it became the task of the author, with a somewhat different purpose in view, to reorganize and rewrite this earlier report. The reader should bear in mind that at every step the study has rested not on the independent labors or insights of a single investigator, but on the interdependent work of a research staff, including psychologists, physicians, a physiologist, and a school counsellor. It has involved also the patient and long-continued assistance of teachers and parents, and, most of all, the coöperation of those essential participants who were children at the beginning of the study and whose development was observed through adolescence.

Acknowledgments are due to Dr. H. R. Stoltz for contributing data used in the analysis of physical growth, and to Dr. Anna Espenschade for records of physical abilities. Dr. Mary Cover Jones was responsible for the testing program in schools and for other home and school data, and Dr. Genevieve Carter for the assembly of sociological materials on neighborhood and community. While many staff members participated in making observational records, Mrs. Frances Burks Newman, Dr. Caroline Tryon, and the late Dr. W. J. Cameron were chiefly responsible for the organization of this field material. The writer is indebted to Dr. N. W. Shock for the analysis of physiological changes (in Chapter V), to Dr. Nancy Bayley for the portrayal of skeletal maturing, and to Dr. Else Frenkel-Brunswik for the method applied to the analysis of drive ratings. Especially helpful have been the services of Miss Judith Chaffey in her contacts with the subjects and their parents, and in her contributions to staff conferences; she is also the originator of methods illustrated in Chapter IX, for the analysis of inventory items and reputation judgments.

The following staff members were responsible for initial drafts of material included in certain sections of this report: Dr. Mary Cover Jones, Chapters I, II and VII; Mrs. Frances Burks Newman, Chapter IV; Dr. N. W. Shock, pp. 76-80; Dr. Else Frenkel-Brunswik, pp. 116-119; and Miss Judith Chaffey, pp. 133-139 and 142-151. Acknowledgment is also gratefully made to Mr. L. K. Frank, Miss Wilma Lloyd, Dr. Lois Meek Stolz and Dr. H. S. Conrad for suggestions and criticisms at various stages in the study, and to Dr. R. J. Havighurst for numerous helpful suggestions based on his teaching experience with an earlier version of the report.

The major study, of which this was a small part, was financed through grants from the Laura Spelman Rockefeller Memorial and the General Education Board.

HAROLD E. JONES,
Director, Institute of Child Welfare,
University of California

No understanding of general laws is possible without some degree of acquaintance with particulars. If we assume that the concrete and the general are of equal importance in the production of psychological understanding, it follows that case materials (including personal documents) should claim half of the psychologist's time and attention. —G. W. ALLPORT

DEVELOPMENT IN ADOLESCENCE

Chapter I

HERE JOHN WAS AT HOME

A. COMMUNITY AND NEIGHBORHOOD

As far back as he could remember, John Sanders had lived in West Town at 161 54th Street, in the middle of a block of small homes. He attended his neighborhood school, daily walking or, later, riding a bicycle, along the same fixed circuit from home to school and back again. Sometimes but not often he deviated from this familiar course to follow some passing interest, or to visit a friend who, like himself, had always lived in the same neighborhood. In the afternoon there were errands to do for his mother at various nearby stores. On Sundays he walked alone to the Sunday school on Pinkham Avenue a few blocks away.

Within this small radius—the school, the store, a friend's back-yard, Sunday school—John had a sense of belonging; he had traveled these routes by himself since he had started to school in the first grade. He was more alone and more restricted in his neighborhood comings and goings than were most of the boys. His mother rarely accompanied him, yet he felt the weight of her presence in her anxiety to have him home on time and to hear his recital of all the small details of the day's happenings.

Sometimes he and his father met after Sunday school [1] and, a sober pair, went to church together; on rare, prized

---

[1] Five out of six of John's school acquaintances attended either church or Sunday school. Four out of five were Protestants.

1

occasions, they would spend a Sunday afternoon at Uncle Dave's chicken ranch in Pear Valley; or, on the other side of West Town, they would tour the warehouse district where Mr. Sanders shopped among the junk-yards for plumbing supplies. This, however, was almost the sum total of John's wider experience with the world about him; his opportunities to explore were few and always protectively supervised, for Mrs. Sanders was not one to favor adventuring either alone or with friends.

The vigorous commercial enterprises of the large growing city were not visible in John's small living area, and were glimpsed only on those infrequent excursions when he walked with his father toward the industrial district, or ventured by ferry-boat to the still larger metropolis across the bay. On warm days when the wind blew from the waterfront, the smells from petroleum refineries, tomato canneries, and a coconut oil plant, along with the distant sounds of trains and ships, reminded John of the activities of the city which lay sprawled out to the west. Toward the east, on wide reaches of hills, were the homes of the more prosperous residents of West Town, spaced with green lawns, sheltered with trees, and built to command a view of the teeming city and the harbor below.

Four thousand dollars would have bought outright the average home in West Town, and $26.00 per month would have sufficed for an average rental, during the depression decade of the 1930's. These figures for West Town as a whole applied also to John's neighborhood, where two families out of five owned their own homes. Figure 1 shows the relation of this neighborhood (District C) to various features of urban life. Midway between the residential and industrial districts, it occupied a slightly faded but very respectable section of the city. It was in the reduced tempo of this middle class environment, and in the quiet restraint of his

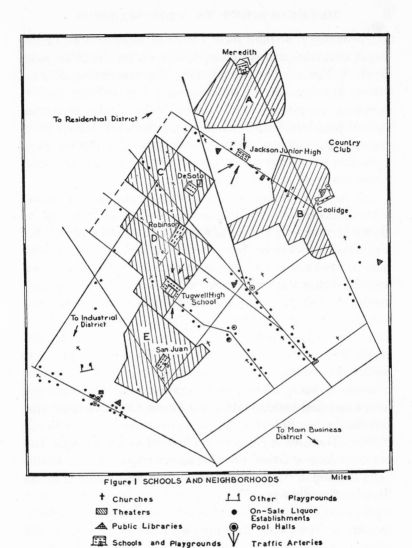

Figure 1 SCHOOLS AND NEIGHBORHOODS

Miles

† Churches	⌐⌐ Other Playgrounds
░ Theaters	● On-Sale Liquor Establishments
⛰ Public Libraries	◉ Pool Halls
⌂ Schools and Playgrounds	⋁ Traffic Arteries

FIG. 1.—SCHOOLS AND NEIGHBORHOODS

life at home, that John received his first impressions of the social structure into which he was expected to fit his own conduct. The small houses adjoining the Sanders home, compactly built on lots of uniform size, reflected the nondescript urban styles of the early 1900's. Each house had its metered city conveniences; each had the luxury of a backyard, a jumbled area held together by clothes-lines; each had some attempt at a front lawn, with an occasional brave clump of shrubs and flowers.

As shown in Figure 1, John's home in the DeSoto district was some distance away from the major concentrations of liquor stores and pool halls. It was also safely remote from the three heavy delinquency areas of the city; when John was in the sixth grade, guidance records included only one case of delinquency at his school, while elementary schools nearer the industrial district reported fifteen or sixteen times that number. In various other indices of the "general goodness" for living,[2] such as the infant mortality rate and communicable disease rates, John's neighborhood stood well within the average of the city as a whole.

There was a sprinkling of foreign names in the school and in the neighborhood. Among the Allens, Greens, Millers and Thompsons could be found also an occasional Capri, Melnik, Velker. There were no Jewish children in John's class, and no Negroes nor Orientals.[3] For the most part, those parents who had come from the old country were natives of either Italy or Scandinavia.

The neighborhood was not one in which boys were forced to play on the street. In addition to their own back yards,

---

[2] "General goodness" is the term Thorndike uses for factors which make up a good community. E. L. Thorndike, *Your City* (New York, Harcourt Brace, 1939), p. 204.

[3] The city population by the 1930 census was ninety-six per cent white, two-and-one-half per cent Negro, one-and-one-half per cent Oriental.

they could make use of a large city playground only a few blocks away; or, in more familiar surroundings, they could use the play areas around the school, where directed recreation was provided after school and on Saturdays and holidays. But for various reasons John seldom entered into these group activities. One reason was the constant pull of home duties—household chores, and errands to run for his mother.

B. JOHN'S MOTHER

John was eleven years old and in the fifth grade when Miss Colby visited his home to enroll him in the "Growth Study." John's mother seemed coöperative, and while only mildly curious about the purpose of the study, was glad to chat with a visitor. Miss Colby announced that all of the fifth graders in John's school, and from four schools in other districts, were invited to join the study; our aim, she explained, was to make a record of the normal course of development rather than to provide detailed guidance; a school counselor, however, was a member of the staff and would be available to talk with John or his parents whenever needed.

Mrs. Sanders, sitting in the only comfortable chair in a clean, but somewhat disorderly living room, responded in a voice that seemed chronically tired, "Perhaps you can tell us what to do about some of John's problems. His father doesn't seem to mind it much, but John is *so* fussy about his meals, and I don't like his dawdling when I give him work to do. I have to be strict with him sometimes. I don't know what makes him as touchy as he is, it doesn't take much to hurt his feelings."

In appearance, John's mother had some of the gauntness which Grant Wood portrays in his "Daughters of the American Revolution." She did not have their severity of expression; her smile came easily, but it was not warm. She laughed

frequently but not heartily; the usual indications of cheer-
fulness or affability seemed in her case to be mannerisms
rather than expressions of immediate good-nature. One
gathered that she was a dominating figure in her own household, and that John, her only child now living at home, was
rarely permitted to forget her demands. Mr. Sanders felt that
his wife "checked up" on John too much for John's own
good, but, in the details of managing the child as well as the
household, it was usually Mrs. Sanders who had the last
word.

Of mixed English and Scotch descent, Mrs. Sanders had
spent her childhood on a remote Idaho farm. Perhaps this
rural upbringing was one reason for her poor success in
establishing a place for herself and for her family in the more
urban surroundings of West Town. Her schooling had
stopped at the eighth grade, and although she gave an impression of alert intelligence, there were few indications of
intellectual interests. Her reading was confined to women's
magazines and a monthly pamphlet published by a Baptist
missionary society. Neither she nor Mr. Sanders "read books."
John, on the other hand, was a frequent and appreciative
patron of a near-by branch library.

C. JOHN'S FATHER

John's father was not without admirable qualities; it
must have required a goodly amount of Christian fortitude
to maintain the rôle which had been assigned him in a household presided over by so determined a wife. He was recognized and approved so long as he contributed to a situation
which allowed his wife to be in unquestioned command. If
these are the submissive traits of a "Casper Milquetoast,"
they are also, by another name, a warrant of loyalty, patience
and forbearance. The son of a small-town hardware dealer

in Nebraska, Mr. Sanders had come to West Town as a young man to work on ships during the first world war. His formal education extended through nine grades, which was about the average amount of schooling for this neighborhood group. He had also taken trades courses which enabled him, one year before his marriage, to set up in business as a plumber.

Like many small business men of mediocre ability and training, Mr. Sanders' earnings were too erratic to give his family financial security. In the boom period (1929) he sometimes made as much as five hundred dollars a month; his annual income of over four thousand dollars was exceeded by only about 15 per cent of the families in the study. When money could be saved he bought oil stocks as investments, with the optimistic conviction that they would provide a later source of income. The depression years, however, brought drastic and totally unlooked-for changes to the Sanders family as well as to most of their neighbors. The 1933 income dropped to one-quarter of its former size; the family could no longer hire a maid, and painful retrenchments in many directions were necessary. The oil furnace and gadget-encumbered hot water heater which he had so proudly installed in his own home were now too costly to maintain. He could not find it in his heart to sell them, and so they remained as symbols of a more prosperous and mechanized era, while he and his wife withdrew their living space into the restricted comforts of the kitchen. The investments which remained of any value were sold to pay taxes. Insurance was borrowed on, and subsequently a number of the policies were lost through inability to meet payments. For a brief period, Mr. Sanders was on government relief.

While many others shared similar difficulties, Mr. Sanders' financial decline was steeper and more bitter than that of the majority of the families in the study. For some of his neighbors, unemployment brought more time for congenial forms of recreation, but this was not the case with Mr. Sanders. He had long since resigned his membership in the Elks, and the family's 1922 Studebaker was no longer equal to the mountain trips which he had occasionally taken during the hunting season. If he could not earn money during the depression, he could at least show his good intentions by working at home, closely supervised by his wife. Mr. Sanders became a conscientious though not a rejoicing handy man about the house.

D. EARLY DEVELOPMENT

In this household, centered about the idiosyncracies of the mother, John became a docile, well-trained child, giving little trouble, requiring little attention. His mother reported that toilet training was very easily accomplished at an early age. In later infancy he spent many hours sitting quietly in his play pen; with little encouragement to creep and explore, he was slow in developing locomotor skills. John was nearly seventeen months of age before beginning to walk—from three to four months later than the average among West Town children.

While John's surroundings were not likely to give him an exaggerated notion of his own importance, nor his relations to his mother a feeling of warm affection, he was not a neglected nor an unappreciated baby. He was encouraged in quiet activities, such as drawing, and given play equipment which would not be too "stimulating." Mrs. Sanders indulged him, within limits, in his whims concerning what clothes he would wear, provided him with clean, comfortable surroundings, adequate food and medical care. She seems to have enjoyed his company.

From day to day, John's mother checked up on what he

did, what he ate, how he looked. She insisted upon his eating properly, and watched his health with anxious solicitude. It was his own idea to be finicky about food, though his mother admitted that she had set him an example in this regard. He refused vegetables unless they were cooked in particular ways; some common foods he refused altogether. It was not necessary to force John to be clean about himself and his clothing. In these respects he was almost incredibly painstaking. In the grade school he was far more interested in his clothes than most of his classmates, who as a rule preferred to look slightly unkempt.[4]

Although John's formulas for manners were not perfect, he was not more ignorant in this sphere than most of the boys and girls in his neighborhood group. He thought it correct "to pass toothpicks at the end of a meal" but knew that it was "not proper to cut up all of one's meat before beginning to eat," and that "soup should be taken from the side of the spoon."[5]

Early in elementary school, his family made the usual gesture toward a cultured education by having John start music lessons. His instrument was the violin; lessons were taken inexpensively, or gratis through the school music department. These were continued until his last semester at junior high school, though a good deal of urging was necessary to achieve the requisite practicing. But at this time music interested John very little, and he presently developed sufficient resistance to drop it completely. The family also

---

[4] Among twelve-year-old boys the reputation for being unkempt was found to correlate positively with many traits having a prestige value. In later adolescence, by the age of 15, this correlation became clearly negative. C. M. Tryon, "Evaluation of Adolescent Personality by Adolescents." *Monographs of the Society for Research in Child Development,* Vol. IV, 1939, pp. 15-16.

[5] Burdick Apperception Test. H. Hartshorne and M. May, *Studies in Deceit,* Vol. I (New York, Macmillan, 1928), xxi, 414 pp.

followed social usage in sending John to dancing school. In view of the emphasis upon dancing in the adolescent culture, it is likely that if John in his pre-adolescent years had become a moderately adequate dancer, his later social relationships would have been easier at many points. But he lacked, at this time, any strong motive to learn, and feeling awkward and ill-at-ease on the dance floor, he soon withdrew from the class.

Chapter II

INTO ADOLESCENCE

A. ELEMENTARY SCHOOL

As a public elementary school, De Soto reflected the cultural characteristics of the neighborhood. Like John Sanders, the children who attended were, chiefly, from families who felt that they belonged in this part of West Town. More ambitious parents with an eye to social achievement sometimes enrolled their children in a public school nearer the country club, where they could associate with children from "better" homes. Boys inclined toward mischievous enterprises were occasionally sent in the opposite direction to a public school in the industrial district, where the principal, Mr. Parran, was reputed to have stern and vigorous ways of handling difficult youngsters. Enrolling a child in a private institution was practically unheard of in John's neighborhood, although at later ages a few pupils were attracted to parochial schools or to privately operated schools in West Town or in the neighboring college community. At school as at home John was in an atmosphere dominated by women. Miss Alden, the principal, was a little gray-haired woman past middle-age—orderly, kindly, conscientious to the point of fussiness, unpretentious, "old-maidish," devoted. Like the principal, the teachers were all women, kindly rather than friendly, conscientious rather than stimulating. Those under middle age were a little more spirited, but the whole tone was one of quiet, restraint, precision. In addition to the staff

11

of seven or eight efficient older women, the school offered "practice teaching" to an unending series of students in training. Although John and his classmates might be naturally more attracted to these younger women, in their rôle as teachers they were tentative, afraid, preoccupied. They brought to the school an atmosphere of change and of uncertain discipline which somewhat counteracted the quiet efficiency of the regular teachers. For high-spirited youngsters like Allen and Lonny, who sat near John in the classroom, a student teacher's insecure methods were sometimes a challenge to mischief. For boys of quieter mold, like John, the effect was less direct, but with them also there was often a pervading sense of unrest. While the total teaching situation was moderately effective, the learning process brought little outward pleasure to those who shared in it.

There were occasional breaks in the academic monotony; a Christmas play, a spring pageant at Easter, and quite exceptional revelries at graduation time. For those who took part, it was an exciting event to be seen by parents and younger brothers and sisters in the unaccustomed glory of a platform appearance. To the more experienced onlooker these performances appeared mediocre, but for many of the children they provided a gratifying escape from routine.

The disciplinary methods used in the school were mild and somewhat unimaginative. The usual procedure with offenders against classroom order and quiet was to banish them to some outer void, presumably to think over the error of their ways. As a result of this treatment, frequently administered, Allen's mother complained that he had little opportunity to learn what was being taught, since he was required to spend so much time in a state of fidgety exile in the cloak-room, the hall, or the principal's office. Occasional conflicts, however, did not prevent the pupil-teacher relationship from being, as a rule, a respectful and considerate one. The children's relationships to each other were similarly tolerant. Of the five elementary schools included in this study, the De Soto school seemed characterized by a little more gentleness, tolerance, and by fewer evidences of a harsh, competitive spirit. This was partly due to the personnel of the classroom itself. A staff observer commented:

The pet of John's class was Vincent, a small, enthusiastic, friendly, disarming, Italian boy. In spite of his slender build and gentle manner, he was regarded by classmates as a good fighter, and "full of pep." Vincent's prominence, however, was chiefly due to his likeableness rather than to other qualities. To him might well be attributed some credit for the tolerance exhibited among his classmates.

Another member of the group who influenced its attitudes was Emily, a girl whose very presence played upon the sympathy of her associates. She was a blonde, rosy-cheeked, shabbily dressed youngster with a distinct aptitude in art, and a breath of scandal in the family background. As ever, the destitute artist appealed to the group. She throve upon their pity and their admiration. In fact, she clung to this rôle of abused and neglected genius so consistently that her friends began to suspect, in her later school years, that she would be lost without it, and that their efforts in her behalf must therefore go forever unrewarded. It was Emily with whom John most often shared the reputation among his classmates for being sedentary, unfriendly, unsociable, afraid, and in general lacking in spirit and rapport. As they tended to think of Vincent for all the pleasant traits, they tended to think of John and Emily for many of the unpleasant ones.

Alice, another neighbor of John's would have been a conspicuous member of any classroom. Inwardly laden with hostility and aggression toward adults, uninhibited and unstable, she, nevertheless, had mature insights about others, and was surprisingly and unashamedly kind at times to the downtrodden. Even then recognized by her classmates as outstanding in social traits, Alice rose to preëminence as a leader in junior high school. In later years when her influence had waned with the majority, she still continued to represent prestige to John and his associates.

It is apparent that John was not an especially noticed or especially favored member of this school environment. The boys with whom he occasionally played were also for the most part little noticed by their classmates. In the class as a whole, John lacked the social and also the athletic talents to maintain any sort of prestige status. But among smaller groups of acquaintances, who were not overly competitive, who could appreciate his strong points and were not too unsympathetic in exposing his defects, a tolerable existence could be managed. In fact there is ground for believing that at this time his school offered John more satisfaction than did other areas of his environment.

In his last year at the De Soto School, we know that John's classmates thought of him as talkative and restless, but equipped with a sense of humor. They believed that he preferred reading rather than active games, and that in a conflict with others he would give in rather than fight. They considered that he liked to be alone, and that he found it difficult to make friends.[1] There is little evidence that his teachers paid him more regard than did his classmates. He was rarely singled out to take responsibility or to receive commendation. Unlike Karl, who was one of the more mature of the sixth graders, John was never asked to help maintain order in the halls or on the playground among the younger children, or to serve the principal on important errands. Also, unlike his friend Allen, he had never been a disciplinary problem, and it was never necessary to send him to Miss Alden's office for special measures. Less often noticed than most of his classmates, John probably was not aware of any direct influence of the principal, yet the individual atmosphere of the school (so apparent to the observer), the ways in which it showed spirit and the ways in which it lacked spirit, were to a large degree an expression of Miss Alden's own personal characteristics.

Although his teachers gave him little special attention, they knew the details of his home background and were sorry for him. They knew that his mother was not always

---

[1] The source of this evidence is described in greater detail in Chapter III.

"easy to live with"; that his father was a skilled worker, out of work; that he was a "socially only child" (one sister, much older than he, was married and living in the East); that John himself was overburdened with cooking and cleaning and errands; that his health had been delicate. All these things each teacher knew and in turn passed on to the next when John was promoted. These teachers must have observed, also, that John was often ill at ease with his classmates, awkward in games, and alone. But the final report about John, sent on by his sixth grade teacher, did not mention his lack of physical skill or social ease. Presumably such defects were not then looked upon as formidable handicaps. Our observers' first notes about John stress the point that although he was clumsy at games, this did not seem to bother him to a marked degree. While he was one of the loneliest he was also one of the most independent boys in the school group. In keeping with his physical limitations, he had developed interests in drawing, reading, and collecting stamps which gave him dependable satisfactions.

B. JUNIOR HIGH SCHOOL

When he was twelve-and-a-half, John graduated from his accustomed elementary school surroundings into the seventh grade at Jackson Junior High.[2] Now he traveled a little farther afield on his way to school. No longer a member of a small unit of 200 children, all from a somewhat similar socioeconomic background, he found himself in a much larger, more variegated group. He met in his classes boys and girls from less substantial, less financially secure sections than his own; he also came in contact, for the first time, with children from well-to-do homes in the hill districts. There were one or

---

[2] The Jackson School, and the five grade schools tributary to it, are shown in Figure 1.

two Negroes, a few Chinese and Japanese in the group, but it was predominantly a group of white Americans of native-born parents. A casual observer would have noted few evidences of "dressing up" in the clothing of the boys and girls attending this school. The boys wore long "cords" or "jeans," [3] cotton shirts and sweaters. The girls wore cotton dresses, sweaters, socks, and rubber-soled "flats," the year round. It was considered "sissy" for boys to own galoshes or rubbers, but boys and girls who could afford it usually had rain-coats, in various stages of jauntiness and dilapidation, which were worn to school on rainy days.

The junior high school building had been planned to provide for 400 students. Now there were over a thousand in attendance. Little by little, portable structures had been erected to take care of the crowding until there were more children housed in portables than in the main buildings. These had inevitably encroached upon the playground space. The portable buildings were poorly lighted, poorly heated and ventilated, and not at all insulated for noise. A perennial administrative problem involved the placing of portables so that "noisy" activities such as shops, orchestra practice, and physical education activities, did not interfere too greatly with regular classroom teaching.

At the time when John entered Jackson, the school authorities were trying to adjust the curriculum to what were regarded as the "needs" of adolescents. Junior high schools have sometimes been criticized as forcing down to the eighth and even to the seventh grade a type of regimentation (as to program and standards) formerly found only at higher grade levels. Aware of this tendency and not fully approving it, the staff at Jackson had undertaken to lighten the program and to allow pupils more opportunity to select courses. One innovation was to offer but not require mathematics in the

---

[3] Corduroy or denim trousers.

eighth and ninth grades. Many parents objected to this as "not giving enough drill on essentials." There were other revisions in the curriculum which occurred while John attended Jackson; some of these changes affected him very directly. In recognition of superior work, John was invited to join a special group in arts and crafts which met at eight o'clock three mornings a week. He was also advised to take a special class in dancing. In spite of earnest participation in this latter group, John had no great success in learning to dance with the agility and smoothness required by contemporary standards.

Two departures in the physical education program were designed to be of benefit to boys like John. One involved a "mixed" physical education period once each week, planned with the purpose of promoting an easier relation between boys and girls in this period of dawning consciousness of the other sex. The other was a special physical education class in which boys who lacked physical strength or skill could be given added attention and practice at their own level of ability. John was a member of this unit.

The recreational program of the school was promoted through assemblies and school plays which to a large degree were a real expression of the children's own ideas of drama and entertainment. They were often unpolished but usually lively. A highly spontaneous and farcical vaudeville act, presented annually by the men faculty, was a high spot on one "varieties" program. Student-faculty relations tended to be informal and friendly. We have no indication, however, that John felt especially close to any of his teachers.

Jackson was a demonstration and training center for a university school of education in an adjoining city. For the first time in his experience, John was in a school in which some of his teachers were men. He also encountered, as at De Soto, a succession of student teachers, many of whom were baffled by disciplinary problems. The freedom of expression and movement allowed in the "progressive" tradition of Jackson was sometimes an added burden to teachers unskilled or inexperienced in holding the interest of their pupils.

In the seventh and eighth grades, classes were sectioned into four groups on the basis of intelligence. John was placed in the second from the highest, composed of children with intelligence quotients from about 100 to 115. In his first semester only seven of his former acquaintances from the De Soto School were in his classroom. Karl was there; also Vincent, the leader of his old group; and Wayne, an earlier friend. The three others were girls who were not of especial importance in John's environment. Vincent and Karl were less influential here than at De Soto, and Wayne was not especially well liked. John now came in daily contact with Ralph Souza, who later became his best friend.

The opening of the Clubhouse [4] in connection with the Adolescent Growth Study was of immediate interest to John. He attended as often as he could, during noon hour and after school. Punctually at the noon recess he appeared at the Clubhouse, carrying a paper bag of sandwiches. The sandwiches being hastily disposed of, he then had time to read magazines or to play a game of dominoes before the bell rang for afternoon classes. Since John attended regularly and eagerly sought to be included ("How can I get into all the activities that are going on?"), the Clubhouse must have been a source of satisfaction to him. As we shall see in a later chapter, it also brought him many experiences of social failure and frustration.

Another significant event during this period was John's somewhat adventurous decision to join the Boy Scouts. The

---

[4] Observational data from this source are presented in greater detail in Chapter IV.

Scouts brought him into closer contact with a number of boys in the neighborhood, and with one of these (Allen, an earlier acquaintance in elementary school) he even struck up a casual sort of friendship. Allen, however, was too unstable, too preoccupied with his own problems, to provide any very dependable relationship.

Mrs. Sanders felt that the group exploited John, giving him all the hard work to do, such as typing notices, but not awarding him positions of honor. Toward the end of junior high he was put in charge of arrangements for troop excursions. But this also, Mrs. Sanders felt, was too much work, a form of exploitation. The experiences and benefits which John could derive from service to others (except herself), were apparently not highly valued by Mrs. Sanders.

All through this junior high school period, John tried periodically to earn money by selling flavoring extracts and other household items. He heartily disliked this occupation, which was a little out of the accepted line of junior high school employment for boys. Popular jobs at this age were usually those of delivering papers, passing out advertising circulars, selling magazines, or taking care of lawns and gardens. The best of these assignments were usually seized by boys more enterprising and energetic than John.

Mrs. Sanders reported that he never played group games in the neighborhood after school because he was very poor at sports and didn't like to do anything at which he wasn't good. She could remember only one party that John had attended in junior high school; this had been given at the Clubhouse by a girl in his class. He seldom brought friends home unless it was in connection with an occasional Scout errand. In fact his mother reported that he hadn't any special friends.

This lack of friends, both among boys and girls, was a source of concern to his mother, who thought it might be

due to the fact that he had little experience in social relationships at home and could hardly be expected to bring
friends to his crowded unattractive quarters. While partly
determined by economic factors, one suspects that John's
restricted environment was also an expression of his mother's
somewhat limited view as to the activities appropriate to a
boy in early adolescence.

Though John continued to accept his rôle as a stay-at-
home, there were some indications of increasing independence. Toward the end of junior high school his mother
complained that he was beginning to be critical and stubborn. She admitted that due to various worries she herself
was at this time often peevish and irritable. It does not
appear, however, that she could regard with objective tolerance the preliminary signs of John's adolescent rebellion; to
her, these changing attitudes were a source of irritation and
were apparently not thought of as related to her son's social
maturing.

C. SENIOR HIGH SCHOOL

Shortly after his fifteenth birthday, John graduated into
Tugwell High School. He now found himself a forgotten
man in a school twice as large as the one he had left. The
incoming low tenth grade of over 300 pupils included many
of John's classmates from Jackson, but they were widely
scattered in a variety of courses (only one course was required); in any one class John saw only one or two of his
former acquaintances. The new school was not merely be-
wilderingly large, but more complicated than junior high
school in its social structure. John encountered more negroes; [5] more children of foreign born parents, including
Orientals; more children of parents who were in the lower

---

[5] Of the total school population of West Town, 2.4 per cent were Negroes,
2.5 per cent Mexicans, and 2.5 per cent Orientals.

occupational brackets or were on relief. This was because of the location of the school in a less prosperous neighborhood than either the De Soto or Jackson districts. To John, going to school in the morning now meant riding his battered bicycle through a poorer section of town rather than toward the hills and better homes. But Tugwell also attracted children from families of high cultural and economic levels; many of these came from other sections of town and from neighboring communities, attracted by the fact that this was a "progressive" demonstration school with the greatest social prestige of any high school in the city. The school administrators accepted and perhaps encouraged this heterogeneity in the belief that contacts of widely differing groups would have a broadening effect and be conducive to liberal attitudes. In some quarters, especially among girls, and still more especially among the mothers of girls, the presence of so many members of "socially distant" groups was felt to furnish an element of danger. Steps were taken to insure meeting the "right" students—those from homes with similar standards and goals.

Invitational social clubs were the principal means employed by socially anxious or ambitious students to insure themselves a comfortable good time through their high school days. None of John's immediate acquaintances "made" any of these clubs, so that he was not directly affected by them. However, the pattern of sophisticated entertainment set by many of these groups—large dances in country clubs or in the hotels of nearby cities—discouraged the simple home parties which had flourished in junior high school days. Similarly, school dances which must be over at eleven-thirty could not compete in appeal with those outside of school which lasted until small hours, thus allowing the high school group to emulate their university neighbors by getting home toward morning.

Boys like John, who had been gradually and painfully acquiring the necessary techniques for the simple social affairs encouraged in junior high school, now found that such opportunities were seldom offered. Social discouragements doubtless occur in any group moving from the upper grade in one school to a beginning status in another. However, in this situation the contrast was particularly striking between those who were taken into clubs (and thus given an opportunity to function socially on a par with upper classmen) and those who were left to find their own way. Since only one pupil from Jackson was admitted to a social club this semester, the feeling was expressed by John and his former junior high school classmates that the well-to-do students from other districts "ran the school and the social life of the students" and that those from Jackson hadn't a chance in school affairs.

Later, in looking back over the situation, John was inclined to think (perhaps too optimistically) that he could have gained more recognition if he had tried a little harder.

Money ... it's not the money itself, but if your family has money you meet different people. ... One thing a fellow can do is to be seen at the right places during noon-hour. The "clique" eat at Antoine's, others—the intelligent ones—bring their own lunches. Those who want to belong to the clique eat where they do. I guess I could have belonged, but I didn't work at it.

The social stratification encountered in high school affected the girls much more than the boys. Yet it was the boys more than the girls from Jackson Junior High who were outspoken about the treatment which they received at the hands of the cliques. Although certain positions (such as student body president) were available to students who were not members of these exclusive groups, other offices dealing with the school social functions were traditionally filled by a "club" member.

As far as avenues of approach to these cliques were concerned, John was evidently in many of the "wrong" ones. Chiefly these "wrong" alleys had to do with money, family status, the neighborhood he lived in and the junior high school attended. With superior personal qualifications, however, an individual, especially a boy, could thread his way to success in spite of these social handicaps. John's classmate Karl, from his neighborhood and from the same elementary and junior high school, became one of the accepted leaders of the student body. But John as we know did not have the necessary personal qualifications to overcome other handicaps.

During his tenth grade, John's organized social life was confined mostly to the literary group at the Clubhouse, the Current Events Club at school, and the Scouts. In the twelfth grade he dropped the Scouts and joined the Y.M.C.A. and the Round Table; this latter was a group of serious-minded students who met after school under the leadership of a liberal English teacher, to discuss school affairs, politics, religion, and other topics useful for controversial purposes. In this group intellectual interests were of primary value; though the members were looked upon as queer by the socially élite, they respected each other and were appreciated by the teacher-advisor. That John's social life was still meager, is indicated by his regular attendance at the High School Clubhouse, and his presence at all the parties and excursions offered by the staff. Although he continued to be the butt of practical jokes and a stimulus to teasing remarks, his ability to "take it" came to be respected by members of the group who had grown more tolerant of "different" behavior.

At home there were a number of changes during John's high school days. Finances improved and the family bought a new car, discarding the ancient model that had served them for nearly twelve years. John learned to drive, but had very little opportunity to use the car. His mother, in explaining her strict rules in this matter, indicated that John might "take advantage" if given a chance and so they were always "on guard." She spoke of John's babyhood, and recalled early episodes of alleged stubbornness and self-assertion. Mrs. Sanders complained that John's relationship to his parents was less companionable than it had formerly been.

To look back over John's senior high school career, we know that he continued to be restricted in his social activities. As before, this was partly owing to lack of funds, partly to maternal control, partly to his own physical appearance and other personal inadequacies. In this school for the first time he came up squarely against a situation in which the factors of family, neighborhood, finances and a "typed" personal attractiveness had fairly explicit values. As with most of his classmates, it gave him pause. However, he was courageous enough to face some of his shortcomings and to work to improve himself. He hunted opportunities for mingling with people, and for the most part managed to stand his ground when others felt inclined to ridicule or rebuff him. The effect of this social rejection was somewhat softened when he came to win the support of a few friends in his later high school years.

In spite of these gains, John was by no means considered to be a "regular fellow" by his classmates, nor a "good prospect for college" by the majority of his teachers. When John left senior high school, after three-and-one-half years, he was still an adolescent facing a strange and sometimes terrifying world, and carrying more than a usual portion of conflicts and anxieties. But through his unrelinquished will to amount to something, and to bring order and meaning into a somewhat confused life, he was beginning to make progress

toward a more integrated use of the resources at h
mand.

In the chapters to this point, an attempt has been mad
to present some of the features of John's physical and social
environment, and to sketch a picture of John's own characteristics as they were seen during adolescence. The details
of this picture will be given in more explicit form in the
chapters to follow.

Chapter III

JOHN AS SEEN BY HIS TEACHERS
AND CLASSMATES

A. SCHOLARSHIP RECORD

The record of John's earlier school work is limited to a simple ledger of attendance and grades. If his elementary school teachers had any special knowledge of John, any understanding that would have been helpful to those who were to teach him and counsel with him later, we have little evidence of it in the cumulative folder that accompanied John to his junior high school. Perhaps one reason for the comparative silence about John is that he was well adjusted in the sense of not making any trouble for his teachers. It was the more extroverted, vigorous and assertive youngsters who were likely to be regarded by their teachers as only "fair" or "poor" in conduct and in scholarship. His sixth-grade teacher wrote, "John lives in his imagination; a reader of good books; a sweet child." At junior high school he continued to receive an average grade of B. Exceptions were the A's gained in art and creative writing, and the D's and F's that marred his record in two years of French.

John's greatest scholastic handicap in junior high school was in the learning of foreign languages; this difficulty reappeared in senior high school, when a bare passing grade was all that he could make in Spanish, and an F rewarded his baffled efforts in German. His difficulty in learning the spelling and meaning of words seemed greater than would be expected from a boy of his general intelligence. A similar awkwardness was apparent in English classes whenever spelling or accuracy of form was demanded.

As late as the tenth grade, his spelling was little short of atrocious, as may be noted in the following excerpt from one of his test papers. The selection was dictated by John's English teacher, but the form was John's own:

"No error is so noticeable on a writen paper as an error in spelling," said Mr. Smith. "For that reason we are particliy carefull to imploy strogaphers who know how to spell."

Two years later, however, under the pressure of an interest in writing, John's spelling had improved to a surprising degree. His compositions now contained few errors, although his spelling in "pressure" situations, as in tests, still left much to be desired.

On the whole, John's scholarship in senior high maintained the passable but irregular level of the preceding grades. Offsetting an occasional A in art and in social studies, he dropped to D's in mathematics and English grammar, the latter course being one which he disliked almost as much as a foreign language. By his last semester in high school John had definitely decided to go to college; spurred by the imminent need of college credits, he managed to avoid any perilously low grades, but remained still in a zone of mediocre scholarship.

To what should we attribute John's uneven record in school? Certainly not to a general weakness of intellectual interests, for as we shall see in a later chapter he was exceptional in the breadth and vigor and resilience of these interests in a period when they carried very little prestige (compared with social and athletic skills) among the majority of his classmates. John would have liked to have done better in school, but there was too often a touch of the dilettante about his work, a tendency for interests to flag when he was required to do things that were precise and detailed.

B. TEACHERS' COMMENTS

Prominent in the reports of various junior high school teachers were indications that:

1. John had "creative imagination" and special ability in art.
2. His study habits were fair.
3. He resented direction in the home-room.
4. Listed under "disabilities" the following comment was made: "Adenoids affect speech. Although he aspires to be a singer (yes, a singer!) he is completely lacking in everything that makes him acceptable before any group. Needs help badly."
5. Referring to personality make-up: "An individualist—but pleasant. Very serious—sensitive to beauty. Socially, not at all sophisticated. Rather mature philosophy—rather like an old man."

In such comments we find intimations of John's creative ability, his resentment of direction, the discrepancy between his aspirations and reality, his seriousness, his individualism.

At the end of the ninth grade a counselor wrote:

John was not at all popular. It is difficult to tell whether or not he was unhappy. He was matter-of-fact, business-like and impersonal in his manner and had an insatiable intellectual curiosity. He did not seem actively unhappy except in competition with other boys in physical education....

His school work is at present fairly satisfactory, although he had a greater struggle with French than one would expect; conscientious at first, he is now discouraged and hates it. His mother hammers at him to do his homework and to get to school on time.... John has been one of the most enthusiastic students in creative writing.... His persistence and creative ability and impersonal matter-of-fact attitude will probably save the day for him in spite of a certain queerness and lack of popularity.

His other teachers also caught occasional glimpses of John's personal difficulties and of his problems in social adjustment, but they had little opportunity to understand these problems or to plan any effective ways of dealing with them. Interviewed three years after John had left junior high, his teachers showed little agreement in their recollections of him.

The German teacher, in whose class he had struggled so ineffectively, did not remember him. The vice-principal described him as "on the defensive early in junior high school, later not so much." Miss Ballantine, in creative writing, gave a fuller account: "I remember him as an individualist, a non-conformist who didn't fit in with the pattern of junior-high-school boys and girls. He had great creative ability, a real flair." Miss Conrad, his art teacher, remembered him as "having lots of confidence in himself. He really believed in himself and was very ambitious. He seemed to enjoy most his work with pen and ink."

In senior high school the teachers' reports became more frequent and more explicit. Perhaps the chief impression that one gets from the comments at this period is that John was a complex character, difficult to assess, and presenting a very different picture to different teachers. The comments vary from warm endorsements ("He has a wholesome, integrated personality,") to the laconic diagnosis, "Needs social adjustment." There was agreement about his seriousness, but while this impressed some teachers as a very commendable trait others seemed to find it a nuisance. The following contrasting opinions illustrate this: "I was especially interested in the way he continued to think about things that others would have passed over with a comment and forgotten . . ." and "He asks more questions than anyone—part of his seriousness; he isn't satisfied with less than the whole answer. His type of seriousness doesn't 'fit' exactly."

The English teacher referred a little heatedly to his tendency to "argue and fussily demand explanations." The shop teacher noted, "My outstanding impression of John is of his seriousness, and that he hasn't the same idea of humor as others. Also, he passed judgment on people. Others don't unless things are extreme. He seemed to do so all the time. Fair enough, usually. I imagine he never played much on the street corner...."

Repeatedly the suggestion emerges that he was inept in making initial adjustments to a class, but tended to improve in the course of the semester. The physics instructor noted, "Very early in the semester it became evident that John was finding physics difficult. During these weeks his work was rather poor and his attitude somewhat rebellious." He would defend his own errors, and try to put the teacher in the wrong by criticizing his assignments or his accuracy in marking examinations. During the term, however, a noticeable change occurred: "John has now, for many weeks, been studying hard with resulting success. The success has spurred him on and he now contributes generously to recitation and discussion. Comes in for help and uses supplementary material. His attitude is friendly and helpful."

The history teacher stressed John's unusually lively curiosity. She also noted that he was a serious student and had been doing excellent work in the course. His spelling was "below par" but by hard work he had improved noticeably.

The English teacher was less complimentary:

Trying, plods, independent, stubborn, determined to be stupid. He has nothing to do with others except to share paper or to be helpful after another's absence. He makes no social contact. He hounds student teachers to explain. (The teacher was asked to enlarge upon her statement, 'determined to be stupid.') He argued about things that weren't arguable—peculiarities in the English language which I was hardly responsible for. I admitted they were neither sensible nor reasonable but they were there to be accepted. And still he argued. I slaved with him trying to help him. He seemed to want help but at the same time was completely resistant to learning the mechanics of English. He kept on coming for explanations and arguing. If I had allowed it, the other students would have guffawed at his grotesque errors. They didn't, but he must have felt their attitude.

At a later time the same teacher gave a somewhat more favorable view of John, evidently mollified by the fact that he had been able to pass the college entrance examination in English.

Opinions varied widely as to John's actual ability.[1] Some

---

[1] For results from tests, see Chapter VI.

of his teachers felt that his intellectual interests tended to outreach his intelligence, as noted in the comment:

John's comprehension is nothing above average; he is slow in everything he does ... slow in understanding. In creative writing John's ability and intellectual equipment did not come up to his interest. He works beyond his capacity, if anything.

On the other hand, the view was sometimes expressed that John was scattered in his efforts, too easily distracted by side issues, inconsistent in application, and, hence, that his grades were not a good indication of what he could have done if he had really applied himself: "He has more of a struggle than his intelligence would warrant." It is not surprising that this division of opinion led to conflicting recommendations as to John's suitability for college:

"A poor risk as a college student."
"He doesn't seem to do the 'digging' that a college would require."
"Utterly unable to succeed in college."
"John hasn't always worked consistently, but I think he will succeed in college."
"John has developed a great deal during the past year ... I know the quality of his mind; I have no fear of his success in college."

If these observations and predictions by teachers leave us with the feeling that they are too loosely subjective to be useful, we may turn to another, more controlled source of data in which the teachers expressed their opinions in terms of ratings. In the eleventh grade, three teachers who knew him best rated his interest in school work, his achievement, and his probable aptitude for college. They agreed that his interest was markedly above average, but they differed very widely indeed on the other two variables. On a 7-point scale, the ratings ranged nearly from one extreme to the other (from 1 to 6 in achievement; from 2 to 7 in college aptitude). Such differences may be imputed, in part, to elusive and enigmatic qualities in John's personality. Conflicting judgments, however, carry some hazards for the person who is judged; the counseling received by John from these teachers must have involved a confusingly inconsistent picture of his own attainments and of what he could be expected to do.

The opinions expressed above were based for the most part on status at a given time, rather than on developmental changes. It is not common for high school teachers to describe their pupils in terms of development. Their views about individuals have a life cycle limited to the semester or to a single school year. One teacher, however, had observed John throughout his career at Tugwell High, and felt that he could comment on John's improvement in social relationships.

Two years ago he was having difficulties socially and conflicts intellectually and emotionally.... At that time he was "alone" in a mixed group whose interests were quite different from his. When John gave oral reports, the class did not pay much attention... he was much more "uncouth" than he is at present.... But John is no longer timid ... he has made great progress in the ability to organize... commands respect from his peers. He is objective, critical in sizing things up... penetrating in his judgments of people... well-balanced and well-adjusted.

While this may be too favorable and optimistic an interpretation, we shall see from other evidence that at the end of high school John was in fact showing many signs of improved relationships with the world about him. A staff member wrote at this time:

I think of John as a person who may develop into one of the most interesting adults of any of the members of the study. He has such a great determination to make something worth while of himself; he is no longer so muddled about his own difficulties, and is doing something constructive about them.

Later chapters will suggest some of the multiple sources of this trend toward greater personal and social adequacy. It is not apparent that John's schooling was a leading factor in the process, but the sympathy, encouragement and stimulation that he received from a few teachers undoubtedly was a source of support at a critical time in his development. What were the characteristics of those teachers who seemed able (where others had failed) to give John the conditions necessary for effective work in school? They were, it would seem, teachers who were not too disturbed by John's liabilities; they were more concerned with making John feel secure in positive achievement than in making him feel remorseful about the things in which he had failed. John regarded these teachers as his friends, but they were never his "severest critics."

A number of his teachers, however, were in manifest ways more like John's mother—criticizing, demanding perfection. The neatly planned scholastic discipline which they sought to impose was undoubtedly necessary and valuable for many pupils, but John's tendency was to evade this discipline, to resent it, or to be paralyzed by it. It is not surprising that such teachers looked at him through unsympathetic eyes.

C. CLASSMATES' OPINIONS

Did his classmates have a more consistent picture of John than the teaching staff seemed able to achieve? Our knowledge of his reputation among contemporaries is based on a group test,[2] the instructions for which read as follows:

In this booklet are some word pictures of members of your class. Read each statement and write down the names of the persons whom you think the description fits. Remember: (1) Several people may fit one picture. You may write down after each description as many names as you think belong there. (2) The same person may be mentioned for more than one word picture. (3) Put your own name down if you

---

[2] C. M. Tryon, "Evaluation of Adolescent Personality by Adolescents," *Monographs of the Society for Research in Child Development*, Vol. 4, No. 4 (1939), p. 3.

think the description fits you. (4) If you cannot think of anyone to match a particular word picture, go on to the next one.

Two items were used to describe the extremes of each trait. For example, on a trait which may be called "friendliness," each member of the class is invited to write the name of someone who

"is very friendly, has a lot of friends, is nice to everybody,"

and also someone who

"does not care to make friends, or is bashful about being friendly."

Administered annually and, for certain years, semi-annually from the sixth through the twelfth grade, a ballot record obtained in this way (on a series of reputation-traits) tells us what John's fellow pupils thought of him as compared with others of the same grade level. For each trait, scores were computed indicating the percentage of times a given individual was mentioned as having that particular characteristic. These measures were then transformed into standard scores; a reputation at the active or positive extreme was designated by scores ranging from 51 to 80; a reputation on the negative or inactive side of the scale received scores ranging from 20 to 49. A score of 50 indicates that the individual in question is not mentioned on either side of the scale, or (and this is an unusual condition) that he received an equal number of positive and negative votes.

Table 1 presents a summary of the trait descriptions used in the reputation test, together with the average standard score achieved by John in nine administrations of the test, and his range of scores from lowest to highest. The traits are listed in four groups, classified not on any general psychological basis but with regard to John's reputation relative to the average. In the subsequent discussion, a reference to a

TABLE 1

John's Average Standard Score on Trait Descriptions as Revealed by
the Reputation Test (Grades 6-12)

Positive End of Scale: Scores above 50	Negative End of Scale: Scores below 50	John's Scores:	
		Average	Range
Restless: finds it hard to sit still in class; he moves around in his seat or gets up and walks around.	*Quiet:* can work very quietly without moving around in his seat.	53	48–62
Attention-getting: is always trying to get others to watch what he can do or to listen to him tell about all the things he can do.	*Non-Attention-getting:* does not care whether or not he is center of attention.	50	30–61
Talkative: likes to talk a lot, always has something to say.	*Silent:* does not like to talk very much, is very quiet even when nearly everyone else is talking.	49	30–61
Tidy: always thinks about keeping himself clean, neat and tidy-looking.	*Unkempt:* never thinks about how clean he is or whether he looks neat and tidy.	51	38–60
Assured-Class: does not mind reciting in class before visitors, but is calm and composed.	*Embarrassed-Class:* always feels embarrassed or confused when he has to get up and recite before a class when there are visitors.	54	34–80
Assured-Adults: is always ready to talk to grown, people, even those he does not know very well. Sometimes he does the talking for boys and girls who do not like to talk to grown people.	*Shy-Adults:* is shy with grown people whom he does not know very well; he gets someone else to do the talking for him.	42	24–58
Leader: always knows how to start games or suggest something interesting to do so others like to join in.	*Follower:* waits for somebody else to think of something to do and always likes to follow suggestions which others make.	41	20–58

TABLE 1 (*Continued*)

Positive End of Scale: Scores above 50	*Negative End of Scale:* Scores below 50	John's Scores:	
		Average	Range
Bossy: is always telling others what to do, bossing them.	*Submissive:* does not mind being told what to do, does not mind being bossed.	41	20–58
Popular: someone whom everybody likes; others are glad to have him around.	*Unpopular:* someone nobody seems to care much about; people do not notice when he is around.	39	26–57
Humor-self: can enjoy a joke and see the fun in it even when the joke is on himself.	*Humorless-self:* can never appreciate a joke when it is on himself.	43	35–62
Humor-Jokes: likes a good joke, is the first to laugh and always sees the point.	*Humorless-Jokes:* does not care much for jokes or has to have them explained before he sees the point.	33	20–58
Happy: is always cheerful, jolly and good-natured, laughs and smiles a good deal.	*Unhappy:* always seems sad, worried, or unhappy; hardly ever laughs or smiles.	41	20–50
Enthusiastic: always seems to have a good time; seems to enjoy everything he does no matter where it is—in school, on the playground, at a party, everywhere.	*Listless:* never seems to have a good time; never seems to enjoy very much anything he does.	34	20–50
Grown-up: looks and acts older than he really is.	*Childish:* looks and acts rather childish.	41	20–52
Older Friends: likes to be with boys and girls who are older or ahead of him in school.	*Younger Friends:* likes to be with boys and girls who are younger than he is and who are in a lower grade.	40	20–50

TABLE 1 (*Continued*)

| Positive End of Scale:
Scores above 50 | Negative End of Scale:
Scores below 50 | John's Scores: | |
		Average	Range
Daring: is always ready to take a chance at things that are new or unusual, is never worried or frightened.	*Afraid:* is always worried or scared, won't take a chance when something unexpected or unusual happens.	28	20–44
Fights: enjoys a fight.	*Avoids Fights:* never fights but lets the other person have his own way.	26	20–44
Active in Games: plays active games like football and basketball or likes to run and jump and so on.	*Sedentary:* seldom plays active games like football and basketball, prefers to read or to sit and play quiet games.	27	22–43
Friendly: is very friendly, has a lot of friends, is nice to everybody.	*Unfriendly:* does not care to make friends, or is bashful about being friendly.	28	20–43
Good-looking: is thought to be very good-looking.	*Not Good-Looking:* thought not good-looking at all.	26	20–34

trait is usually in terms of a trait-name for the positive end of the scale (for example, restlessness, popularity, etc.).

John's scores were on the average close to 50 in the first group of five traits in this table (restlessness, attention-getting, talkativeness, tidiness, assurance in class). An unusual range, however, is exhibited. It is significant that in such a trait as talkativeness John varied in different semesters from a position in which he was regarded as extremely quiet, to one in which his classmates thought of him as extremely talkative. Fluctuations of this degree [3] are not common; and their presence suggests an unusual lack of

---

[3] From 2 S.D. below to 1 S.D. above the central tendency.

stability either in social techniques or in more basic aspects of social relationship.

In the second group of traits (assurance with adults, leadership, bossiness, popularity, humor) John's average score was definitely on the negative or inactive side, with a range extending from very low values to values slightly above 50. With regard to his sense of humor, for example, John was usually but not always thought of as "humorless."

In the third group of traits (happiness and enthusiasm; maturity in behavior and in friendships) the range moves downward; John's highest scores in these characteristics were at or close to the middle point of 50, and his lowest scores (20) were the lowest in his class.

In the remaining group of traits, involving several of considerable importance from the point of view of social prestige, John was not only low but consistently low in the opinions of his classmates. In this record we find evidence of an extraordinary accumulation of social stigmata. A less favorable, more handicapping reputation would rarely be found. It is interesting to note, however, that John's score in *popularity* was not as low as in some other traits which have considerable prestige value among boys at this age. It is possible that among his classmates as well as among his adult acquaintances, he has been helped by traits which have some redeeming significance, and which are not clearly apparent in this scale. It is necessary to turn to a more complete cumulative record if we wish to study John's reputation in relation to other aspects of his development.

Figure 2 presents age curves for six selected traits. The data are presented in terms of standard scores in which the group average is 50; the shaded areas from 50 to 40 include 1 S.D. below the average. In the top third of this chart, standard scores are shown for activity (a low score designating the inactive or "sedentary" end of the scale) and for

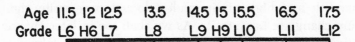

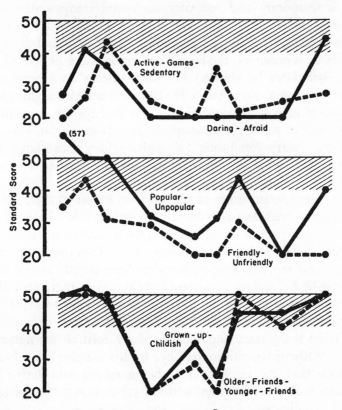

FIG. 2.—REPUTATION WITH CLASSMATES

daring or willingness to take a chance (a low score indicating fearfulness or timidity). We note that John was generally regarded as inactive in games, that is, he received numerous votes as resembling the description "seldom plays active games like football and basketball, prefers to read or to sit and play quiet games." The sporadic rises in the low seventh and high ninth grades do not necessarily signify any change of basic traits. As we shall see in later chapters, apparent athletic interests sometimes served in John's case as a temporary and not very successful compensation for social inadequacies. The low seventh grade was a period when John was plunged suddenly into a new and strange school environment; the high ninth grade was a period when (as will later be shown) he was carrying an exceptional burden of adolescent woes. If at these times he sought more physical activity than usual, this was perhaps less a genuine outlet than a hopeful attempt to gain favor in the eyes of others. John's reputation for activity in games shows no correlation whatever with his expressed preferences as exhibited in an interest test (see Chapter VII).

In the second trait at the top of Figure 2, John was generally considered to be afraid rather than daring ("is always worried or scared, won't take a chance when something unexpected or unusual happens"). Less deviate in the sixth and seventh grades, from the low eighth to the low eleventh he ranked consistently at the very bottom of the group in this trait. In the last year of high school the return toward more normal values is a favorable sign.

What is the social significance of a record of this nature? In a study of seventh-grade boys in this sample, it has been shown that the reputation of being daring and active in games is closely associated with the reputation for leadership and friendliness:

Extreme positive scores imply skill, leadership, and fearlessness in organized group activities, and a friendly cordial manner though a rather aggressive and dominating one; extreme negative scores imply fearfulness and lack of skill in and distaste for organized group games with connotation of social ostracism. Positive scores tend to be rather highly related to buoyancy of temperament and to personal likeableness. Study of extreme cases and also of the statistical evidence points to the interpretation that this is the most prestige-laden cluster for

twelve-year-old boys. At the one extreme boys are admired and respected, at the other ridiculed and shunned.[4]

At the tenth grade level the findings are somewhat similar,
negative scores continue to indicate physical weakness and
the attributes of a "sissy." Positive scores imply a reputation
for skill, bravery, the capacity to "take it," and also, at this
age, some of the attributes of social ease and heterosexual
adjustment.

With such glamorizing values attached to physical activity and initiative, we are not surprised to find John in an
inferior position with regard to popularity. The middle
section of Figure 2 indicates that except in the sixth and
seventh grades he was distinctly on the unpopular side of
the average, reaching a lowest extreme in the ninth and
eleventh grades; he was also generally regarded as unfriendly, "Doesn't care to make friends, or is bashful about
being friendly."

The remaining two curves in Figure 2 illustrate the impression John made with regard to maturity; while at other
ages he was rarely mentioned as being immature in behavior or in his choice of friends, it is worth noting that
during the eighth and ninth grades, between the ages of
thirteen-and-a-half and fifteen, John was quite conspicuously on the less mature side of the scale. We shall see, later,
the relationship of this to our data about John's physical
development. It is also important to note the general opinion
that John was more feminine than masculine in his interests.
A reputation as a "sissy," coupled with a social stereotype of
avoiding fights, being submissive, afraid, and inexpert in
games, is no light handicap for a 'teen-age boy who has an
ambition to be socially accepted.

In his other reputation traits, Table 1 presents little evi-

---

[4] C. M. Tryon, op. cit., p. 36.

dence of any characteristics which would seem to place John in an especially favorable light in the eyes of his associates. Undoubtedly his most favorable record was attained at the beginning of the study (low sixth grade) when he was noted as slightly above average in popularity, average in leadership, and above average in humor and in assurance. From this position his reputation slipped to a low-water mark in junior high school, recovered slightly at his entrance to senior high (when he was less well known by those voting); declined again as he became better known, and then at the end of his high school career showed a promising upward tendency. The reputation gains at the end of his school career appear to parallel the trends in comments of some of his teachers; these gains are probably due in part to changes in the social standards of his peers, who were beginning to place less value upon traits in which John was weak, and at the same time were better able to recognize the merit of John's endeavor in other fields.

In interpreting such records as these, we must of course remember that reputation is not always a faithful reflection of actual traits of behavior. When, for example, a boy avoids others because of shyness, he is very likely to be judged or misjudged as unfriendly. Even when behavior is correctly appraised, a quite minor expression of a trait may at times have an exaggerated echo in the opinions of others. Moreover, this echo may "reverberate," in the sense that it influences judgments about other traits in addition to the one in question. It is also likely to have some return effect upon the subject's subsequent behavior.

In John's case, there was little opportunity to be blissfully unaware of what his classmates thought about him. With the brutal frankness of youth, they had on various occasions addressed him as "worm," "Jackass John," and, in derision of his physical weakness, "Old Ironman Sanders." Such jibes were impossible to ignore, and also not easy to take. Perhaps to some extent he succeeded in softening their impact by making rationalizations about them.[5] But he was not so devoid of insight as ever to believe that his social condition was a fortunate one.

It is instructive to consider the extent to which John's reputation, as it was viewed by his classmates, resembled his behavior as recorded by adults specifically trained in the techniques of observation. This will be considered in the following chapter.

D. GROUP STRUCTURES

Some of the features of the adolescent subculture, of which John was a member, can be seen more clearly in terms of the friendship groupings [6] in John's class, presented graphically in Figure 3. The lower half of this sociogram indicates associations among girls, in the high ninth grade, based on replies to a question about "best friends." Each circle in the chart represents an individual case. A solid line connecting two cases indicates that each has mentioned the other as a best friend. A dotted line indicates a one-way mention, in the direction shown by the arrow. It can be seen that among the girls in John's class the social structure, at this age level, consisted of a number of compact and some-what separated groups or cliques. Group 1, for example (upper left corner), contains seven girls none of whom mentioned anyone outside of the group, although three members were mentioned by outsiders as best friends. Group 2 is a self-sufficient triangle of three girls all of whom mentioned

---

[5] John's adjustments in this area, particularly in the more critical periods of his social development, are considered in Chapter IX.

[6] These relationships are presented in greater detail in H. M. Campbell, *Personality Differences Between Adolescent Boys and Girls Revealed by a Matching Technique*, Ph.D. Dissertation, University of California, 1939.

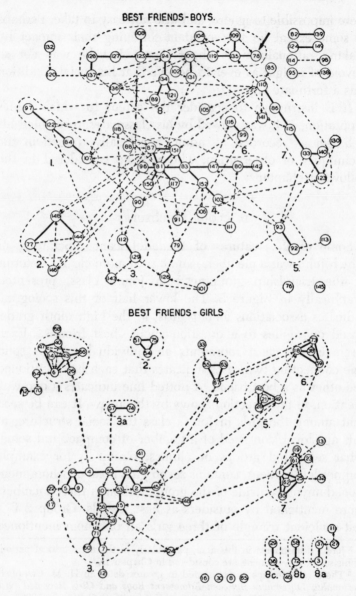

Fig. 3.—Sociograms for Boys and Girls

each other and no one else. Group 3 is a larger and somewhat amorphous aggregation, with a number of outside connections. In the lower right are four girls who had no friends in the school, and admitted it; there are also several "chum-pairs" (group 8 *a*, *b* and *c*) who seem relatively independent.

The upper half of Figure 3, exhibiting inter-personal relationships among the boys, defines a very different social structure. With a less excluding organization, it seems democratically easier for a boy in any group to have some one whom he regards as his best friend in any other group. An arrow pointing toward 78 indicates the position of John Sanders in this sociogram. He mentioned 135 (Ralph Souza) as his best friend, and made no other mentions. Ralph mentioned him in turn, and John was also chosen as a best friend by 109 (Will Haines). Although not at the center of any social grouping, and not recognized by anyone of high social prestige, John nevertheless had more of a "place" in the class than several boys shown on the periphery of the chart.

Six months later, in the low tenth grade, John was "dropped" both by Ralph and by Will. He joined the members of that small and pathetic group who mentioned no one as a friend, and were mentioned by no one. In the eleventh and twelfth grades, however, we find Ralph and John restored as mutual friends. In addition, John had two other friends in the twelfth grade; in terms of his own and his classmates' report, he was now in a less isolated position than at any previous time in our records.

Chapter IV

JOHN AS A MEMBER OF SOCIAL GROUPS

A. BOYS' GROUPS

Each spring and fall small groups of John's classmates came to the University for a physical examination and a series of tests. The waiting room presented an inviting array of play equipment which could be exploited during intervals between test periods, and the Institute playground was available for outdoor activities during the noon hour. In these "free play" situations the staff enjoyed an excellent opportunity for observing personal characteristics of the children, and inter-personal relationships. The observations were recorded in three forms: ratings, narratives, and descriptive comments.[1]

On his first visit a staff observer described John as a rather slim boy with tousled dark hair, a good-natured expression:

The other boys appeared to like him well enough; however, he was the odd man, without a partner. He was inexpert and a little awkward in games with balls, horseshoes, etc.—like an adult who has not played for a long time. He did not seem to mind this—was a little apologetic and a little amused. As a matter of fact, he was quite at home in the Institute—drawing seems to be one of his special abilities, so he enjoyed himself.... He never tried to dominate and yet did not submit

---

[1] During John's school career, a total of 250 observational records of his behavior and social relationship were collected and systematically organized. The observational procedures are discussed in H. E. Jones, "Observational Methods in the Study of Individual Development," *Journal of Consulting Psychology*, Vol. 4, 1940, pp. 234-238.

to bossiness, resisting interference in a firm, good-natured sort of way....

At this time John was eleven-and-a-half years of age and in the low sixth grade. The following verbatim records give more specific impressions of John's behavior in the group of other boys:

John and Allen are working at an easel. John is intent on a picture of an Indian chief. Allen is talking and singing in a high-pitched voice, mixing conversation with snatches of song and dramatic imitations. Allen draws a picture of a boy and girl kissing. . . . "Maybe that will be me some day."
Allen: "Now I'm going to do one of the modest artist"—(draws an artist painting at easel.) To John: "Mix your paint up; it will be better!"
John: "I like mine just as it is . . ."
Allen (*sings*): "Tomatoes are cheaper (etc.); now is the time to fall in love. . . ." Remarks, "They say we're coming up here four times a year. . . . what do we do this for?"
John (*turning to observer*): "So you will be able to tell others how we grow, isn't it—how others grow?"

.   .   .   .   .

John joins others in playing a miniature pin-ball game. He isn't nearly as good at it as the other boys. Between times, he tries other diversions. Plays with a doll, making up a story about mama and children; "Mama is angry". . . .
John: "I'll play you a game of marbles."
Peter: "I've a new idea for a game!" He starts to arrange marbles on the board.
John (*a little irritated*): "Get out of there. I want to shoot!"
Peter (*also irritated—a little bossy*): "Wait a minute, wait a minute!"
John: "Give me my marble back!"
Peter: "I never thought you was such a baby!" He takes first turn at a new game.
John (*good-natured, but aware he is being bossed*): "*You* would, *you* would!"

A very different relationship to his classmates is shown in the following sample records, obtained when John was in the ninth grade:

L 9, age 14.5 years

In the playground with five other boys, John's behavior today illustrates some of the reasons for his present social difficulties.... After a mild amount of physical exertion on the swing, he lay down rather white and drawn-looking. When Art wanted to place a bet on whether he could vault a fence, John looked panicky and then declared he didn't take bets, implying it wasn't a nice thing to do; his manner was slightly belligerent. As soon as it was obvious that Art himself would be unable to perform the proposed stunt, John rushed over and wanted to bet, making a great fuss about it when his offer wasn't taken.

H 9, age 15 years

John was slightly injured in a basketball game when he tripped and fell against a tree. He seemed to react overmuch, in an attention-getting way. When he finally got up, Allen helped to brush off his trousers.... Allen and Ray, in a teasing mood, pushed John into a cart and pulled him around in circles until he gave every sign of being dizzy. Released, he staggered to the side of the yard and put his head down on a box. Allen put his arm around him and asked if he had been hurt. John seemed to recover immediately, and later went back to the cart, almost seeming to invite punishment.

Other comments: John is sometimes shunned, sometimes tolerated by the group. Self-conscious, he hesitates to compete in games. His inadequacies seem to make him self-centered and defensive, but he will not overtly defend himself when attacked or teased....

Two years later, John seemed to avoid situations in which he could be teased or in which he would contrast unfavorably with his classmates:

L 11, age 16.5 years

John impresses one as being rather unsocial, self-contained, capable of following his own interests even when they are in conflict with those of the group. As a rule his interests are individual, rather than essentially antagonistic to those of the group. While the other boys played ball, John sprawled on the ground and talked to staff members about movies, radio programs, and music. In the previous year he had played the Victrola in the waiting room, seeming less interested in the music than in getting unusual effects from it by changing the speed control; by these antics he also succeeded in teasing other members of the group. Now, however, John showed a genuine interest in our selection of records, playing a variety of popular pieces, and announcing quite positively what he liked and didn't like. His tastes were similar to those of the other boys, following closely the current dance band favorites. He differed from the others, however, in being willing to try out classical pieces . . . perhaps more from curiosity than from actual preference.

John is still a completely inconspicuous member of the group, although he seemed to show a bit more independence of spirit today than previously. . . . When the other boys are talking he is completely passive; he doesn't know how to express himself in the boyish, hearty way of the others. He contributes nothing to the conversation; sits and reads while the others are talking. His manner lacks force, and he is still unattractive in appearance. During test situations it is characteristic for him to seem nervous, jumpy, distractible.

In the records made in his senior year John seemed less subject to teasing than in previous semesters, and more acceptable to others although he was still left out of some of the group activities. Following is an episode which contrasts with his withdrawn behavior of a year earlier:

L 12, age 17.6 years

During the noon hour John had little to say at first, but later monopolized the conversation, gave directions and ordered others about. Free with opinions. Persistent, single-track, in pushing an argument. Seemed to identify self with adults . . . indifferent to the social activities of groups. Persisted in putting personal preferences before the group interests. But the group appeared to respect his self-assertion, and Jim Enderby bestowed the favor of choosing him as a partner for one of the test procedures.

These anecdotal summaries provide an overview of changes from juvenile to more mature interests, and also of a significant pattern of changes in John's relationship to others. The evidence which they contribute is convincing only if the reader believes that they represent a fair sample of John's behavior in the situations described. In the case of informal records of this nature, an author may of course incline toward the selection of episodes which emphasize the theme he has previously determined upon. This subjective factor can be reduced if we turn to more systematic records embodied in ratings. The ratings, now to be presented, are based on specific behavior samples observed during the five-hour visit to the Institute. The chief source of observational material was the free play activity occurring on the playground during the noon hour.

Figure 4 presents illustrative year-to-year charts for results based on these ratings.[2] In this as in Figure 2 the raw measures have been transformed into standard scores in which the group average is 50; the shaded areas from 50 to 40 include 1 S.D. below the average. It is readily seen that John's scores were low in all of the traits represented. In "social prestige," "sociability," and "poise," he averaged around a standard score of 30 (that is, 2 S.D. below the mean, or in the lowest 5 per cent of the boys in his class). He was markedly lacking in "buoyance," that is, on specific subtraits he was not rated as cheerful, relaxed, carefree, but as glum, tense, and anxious. In the trait "directness" (a term used to designate matter-of-fact, unaffected behavior) John's low scores in grades 7 to 10 signify that he was "indirect" in the sense of being affected and attention-getting.

If we look for age changes, we find in general an improvement from the seventh to the eighth grade. This is not extended in the ninth grade, but improvement is again shown in grade 10. Grade 11 brings a recession in every characteristic except "directness," while grade 12 shows a return to

---

[2] Each point is derived through averaging independent assessments, by three raters. The trait names shown in Figure 3 are used for convenience in summarizing the data: the traits are not rated as named, but in terms of more specific ratings of subtraits. Thus, "Social prestige" is a composite based on ratings of (a) initiative, (b) leadership, and (c) effect-on-group. The data for grades 7, 8, 9 and 10 represent, in each case, two visits to the Institute (spring and fall); the data for grade 11 and 12 represent single visits.

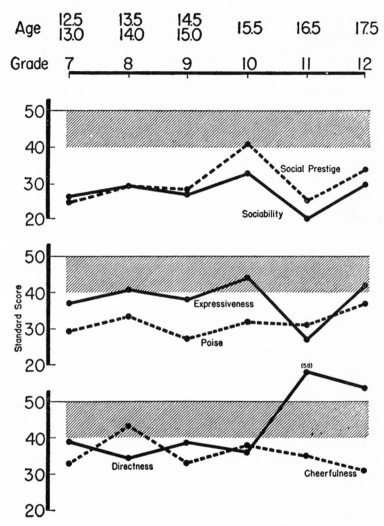

FIG. 4.—RATINGS BY ADULT OBSERVERS (BOYS' GROUPS)

somewhat more normal levels in the social traits and in expressiveness and poise. Similar changes, in grades 11 and 12, have been noted for John's popularity with his classmates (Figure 2).

During the first four years represented here, John's low score in "directness" suggests that he was using attention-getting behavior as an attempt to compensate for his lack of status. He was not, however, using it in such a way as to bring about any effective gains in his position among associates. In grade 11 the attention-getting devices have disappeared. This would not necessarily be a favorable sign, for while it would remove one symptom of maladjustment and one source of irritation to others, it might at the same time indicate a withdrawal from social contacts; this is, in fact, suggested by the accompanying changes in other traits. The partial gains in social traits in grade 12 suggest that new factors have come to John's aid and are helping to reverse an unfavorable trend. What these factors are will be considered in later chapters.

B. BEHAVIOR AMONG BOYS AND GIRLS

The foregoing observations of John's social behavior were made only among groups of boys. Another series of records is available, extending from the eighth to the twelfth grade, and based on "mixed" social activities—dancing parties, excursions, and a variety of casual social contacts at a Clubhouse [3] maintained by the staff. John was frequently present on these occasions, but characteristically in the rôle of a "fringer," as in the following example:

---

[3] Descriptions of the Clubhouse and its program have been given in: H. R. Stolz, M. C. Jones, and J. Chaffey, "The Junior High School Age," *University High School Journal*, Vol. 15, 1937, pp. 63-72; H. E. Jones, "Observational Methods in the Study of Individual Development," *Journal of Consulting Psychology*, Vol. 4, 1940, pp. 234-238.

Grade H 8, age 14

Clubhouse Living Room, Noon. The room is thronged with boys and girls. A radio is blaring the latest dance music. Several pairs of girls are dancing with each other, a few are dancing with boys. For the most part, however, the boys are either watching, or playing cards or checkers. John is one of the watchers, in a small group beside the fireplace.

Art broke away from this group to dance with another boy; he then began pursuing June, dancing with her as often as she permitted; he seemed very eager and pleased with himself.

Tom also had a partner within a short time. He danced continuously, each time with a different partner—apparently as much concerned with the dancing itself as with the girls.

Hal played two games of checkers; with back turned, he ignored or good-humoredly pushed away several girls who made approaches to or "passes" at him. His air of indifference seemed to indicate a complete confidence in his status with the girls; Hal's dancing later, with Joyce, was expert.

John was in but not a part of this melée of activity; he remained on the sidelines, a spectator and not a participant.

Less than two years later we see John in a new rôle:

L 10, age 15.3

At the PTA party, John danced with Florence, Esther and Emily in a very business-like manner. He went into his dance with zest and determination ... seemed to lose a lot of his awkwardness. Very dignified and proper.

But John was not destined to flower into an immediate social success. In most of the social situations in which he found himself he was still marked not by a lack of interest or desire but by a deadening inertia which made it seem as though every social effort were choked by inner resistances. Under very favorable conditions these conflicts could be overcome, and for a time his relationships with others would take on a new glow. But his unskillfulness and lack of self-confidence made it too easy for him to slip backward into a more customary rôle. Neither from his teachers nor his classmates did he obtain, in this period, the continuing appreciation and support that he needed. The harshness and blunt cruelty sometimes found in the adolescent culture are illustrated in such observations as the following:

H 8, Age 14

Allen and Clayton were playing catch with one of John's gym shoes. While John rushed from one to the other, they would toss it back and forth and skillfully keep it out of his reach. John finally started to walk away without it; Tom, watering the lawn, tried to sprinkle him with the hose. Tom (to protesting staff member): "Oh, we're in his scout troop, we understand him."

Pete and Tony succeeded in getting a library book away from John, and threatened to hide it. They paused, in shocked surprise, when John showed signs of beginning to cry. They were obviously both ashamed of him and a little sorry for him when they found he couldn't "take it." Pete approached him rather awkwardly and patted him on the shoulder.

Clubhouse living room. John chose a chair but was told to get out of it because "it belongs to someone out of the room." There seemed to be a coördinated effort to make him uncomfortable, to which he responded in a rather petulant manner.

Clubhouse porch. John came in with his lunch. Asked if someone would play backgammon with him.

Douglas: "I can play but I wouldn't play with you."

Marilyn (to John): "He's beat better people than you." John dropped the backgammon board, and Douglas and Marilyn laughed at him. He was disconcerted, but still remained on the porch and later played a game with Bill. Bill trotted away abruptly as soon as the school bell rang.

John: "I'm always the one that's left to pick things up."

L 9, Age 14.5

Evening party at the Clubhouse. Most of those present are playing a game which involves penalties. John is reading magazines in a corner. Louise is given the penalty: "Go up to the best looking boy in the room and vamp him." When she balked, one girl said, "Oh, you just go up and say 'I love you,' and then give him a kick." Louise looked relieved at the apparent simplicity of this assignment, but still hesitated.

Dorothy: "Say it to sissy-babe John. He doesn't know the difference anyway."

John responded with a sarcastic "Thank you," without looking up from his reading.

In the Clubhouse yard. John rides up on his battered bicycle.

Joe: "Hello, Johnny."

John: "Hi."

Joe: "Aw, don't be so darned stuck up, or I'll knock you off that bike."

Thus, in the eighth and ninth grades, we see John as a recognized target for scoffing and joking, a scapegoat on whom many of his classmates could project whatever feelings of insecurity they might have. In turn, John himself was inclined to tease others (particularly those lower in status) whenever he could do so successfully and without fear of violent reprisal. It may be significant that he sometimes chose for ridicule the *physical* attributes of others—a fact to be considered in relation to his own only too obvious physical inadequacies.

John's immediate response to ridicule varied from passive submission to petulant complaint, and only occasionally took more vigorous form. In no case were his retorts particularly effective in quieting those who tormented him, or in gaining their respect. He frequently seemed to be stubbornly unaware of the kinds of behavior that would be acceptable to the group.

In spite of almost daily humiliations, John showed a persisting eagerness to "belong," to be a member of groups, and to take part in group activities. Rebuffed, or in anticipation of being rebuffed, he would sometimes withdraw to the outer edge of a group, or to the precarious refuge of a book or magazine, but without actually leaving the group situation. It sometimes appeared as though any kind of attention, even unfavorable, was more satisfactory to him than no attention at all. During a fad of playing backgammon he gained a fleeting status through being an instructor to the class president and to a number of other boys who shed prestige wherever they went. The class president, a political whale among the minnows, treated John, for a short time, with patronizing benevolence. But as this reflected glory died away the harsh ridicule seemed to gain momentum, forcing John into almost complete isolation from the group who dominated the social activities of the school and of the Clubhouse. An observer noted at this time:

Sanders is conspicuous only as an underdog. He certainly fails to cut any kind of a figure with the prevailing popular group. In the phrasing used by the youngsters themselves, he has always been considered "queer," and yet he has a certain individuality which causes him to be taken seriously even by the same individuals who are most zealous and impertinent in making fun of him.

With the maturing of group attitudes and manners, and with some changes in John's own behavior, we find that in senior high school he was less often subjected to teasing and other public forms of humiliation. One would like to feel that in this process of growing up his associates were becoming kinder, more sympathetic, more discerning as to the damaging effects of ridicule. With some of John's acquaintances this transition was undoubtedly taking place, but with others the habit of aggressive and contemptuous domination still remained—expressed in more subtle but none the less effective ways. John now had less to fear from the more obvious kinds of persecution, but before reaching his last year of high school he was to face many experiences of being ignored, snubbed, or actively rejected.

With John's entrance into senior high school, it was apparent that he had established neither the close companionship nor the casual group ties that characterized the social relationships of most of his classmates. It is not surprising that he was socially "lost" in his new surroundings, and that he withdrew to some extent from the earlier beginnings he had made in contacts with girls. And yet, even more strongly than in previous semesters, the evidence suggests a persisting strong desire for favorable attention from his classmates.

In John's second term at Tugwell, the Institute staff opened a new Clubhouse near the school grounds. Although many of the boys and girls had already progressed to more sophisticated social interests than could be met at the Clubhouse, John promptly became a regular attendant. The picture of his behavior is not unlike that of a year before, when he was making unsuccessful attempts to gain attention and to identify himself with his classmates, appearing "queer" and unmasculine in facial proportions, physique, and coördination, and talking with greater freedom among adults than among his peers.

Throughout the tenth and low eleventh grades, John's social contacts were limited chiefly to a few boys who, like himself, were not conversant with or particularly successful in the folkways favored by the group as a whole. He was still exerting repeated attempts to join groups, trying to get various boys to talk to him, and gratefully accepting recognition from the few who responded. As for girls, an observer commented:

> John is obviously the kind of person with whom no girl would go out, if she thought she had prestige to maintain. Even girls who are fairly independent in their attitudes toward their social position would feel that they *couldn't* descend to go out with John Sanders! Perhaps the chief reason for this is his lack of a functional familiarity with social patterns; he tries hard to conform to these standards of the adolescent culture, but is still an outsider wistfully looking in.

Several descriptions suggest that John was "unaggressive" and "meek," lacking in sufficient enterprise to make the more vigorous social advances which he had attempted in junior high school. In this we find some evidence of a withdrawal from his more conspicuous bids for attention, and perhaps even a certain attitude of defeat. One observer offered this interpretation:

> John's detachment and reserve may be related in part to an intellectual self-righteousness about his own interests, in comparison with more flexible and socially determined interests of others. He has a certain rigidity of behavior that makes it hard for him to adapt to immediate circumstances, and also an undeveloped awareness of the effects of his behavior on others.

During this darkest period, however, John had the saving support of a friend. In a number of classes he had come in close contact with Ralph Souza, an earlier acquaintance of junior high school days. Ralph was in some respects a more extroverted edition of John himself—with similar interests—but with a quite decidedly positive and outgoing way of expressing these interests. In Ralph, John found a vicarious means of realizing his own inhibited social aims and intellectual enthusiasms.

H 11, Age 17

John and Ralph came to the office today. John, arriving somewhat earlier, was brusque and uncommunicative. When Ralph entered, he became more ready to talk. His manner was tentative, and his voice light and lacking in confidence. Ralph supplied most of the conversation.

· · · · ·

The John–Ralph combination paid us a visit after school. John as usual was a rather uneasy second to Ralph's ready flow of speech—occasionally he offered suggestions in a tentative manner, and then apologetically withdrew them. Seemed quite dependent on Ralph's opinions and decisions.

If continued, this attitude of discipleship could hardly have been very helpful to John. But under the stimulus of Ralph's fluent expressiveness, and with the support of Ralph's genuine liking and confidence in him, John gradually came to play a more equal rôle.

At the same time, John was achieving a closer and more mature relationship with several teachers and staff members. A boy of intellectual interests, with a great need for social approval, might be expected to turn frequently to adults for some renewal of faith in his own status. Except in the case of a few less appreciative and more easily exasperated teachers, John's rapport with adults was more satisfactory than with his own classmates. It is not surprising that in the latter years of school he was rated as "frequently seeking adult company." [4]

These personal relationships appear to have been of genuine importance to John. With Ralph, and with a few adult acquaintances, he became able to express himself almost with Ralph's own facility. This change was, to be sure, apparent only under quite favoring conditions, and he was still frequently noted as ill-at-ease in social contacts. But in the last year of high school an extension occurred in the situations in which he felt secure and successful. This can be noted in the upper section of Figure 5, in which we see an upward turn in "social self-confidence" after the age of seventeen.[5] Although his prestige had improved within certain limited groups, the middle section of this figure indicates little change in John's popularity with the class as a whole. Figure 5 also shows that John was less disliked by girls than by boys; perhaps they were less influenced by his lack of athletic ability, and had fewer reasons for making John a scapegoat. The lower section of this figure indicates a sharp change, beginning in the tenth grade, in John's attention to

---

[4] John's standard scores in this trait rose from 41 in the low tenth grade to 52 in the high tenth and 64 in the low twelfth.

[5] As in Figures 2 and 4, the original ratings have been transformed into standard scores in which 50 is the central tendency of the group; the shaded area includes 1 S.D. below the mean. Ratings cover the high eighth and high eleventh grades, and both the low and high ninth, tenth, and twelfth grades.

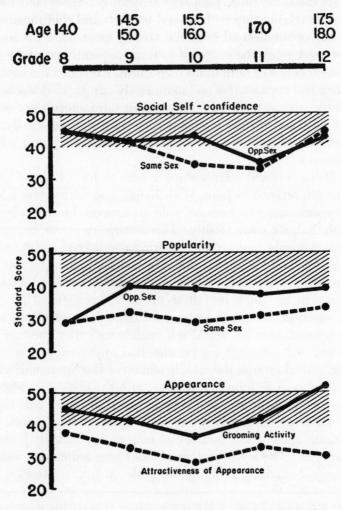

FIG. 5.—RATINGS BY ADULT OBSERVERS (MIXED GROUPS)

"grooming." Often a sensitive indicator of adolescent maturing, the rise in this curve is similar to that of other maturity indices to be discussed in later chapters.

Following is a description of the traits represented in Figure 5. For purposes of comparison with the standard scores in this figure, John's average ratings on a 7-point scale (Grade 12) are given in parentheses after each trait name; the point scores are based on independent ratings by six observers.[6]

TABLE 2

JOHN'S AVERAGE SOCIAL RATING IN THE TWELFTH GRADE AS SCORED BY THREE INDEPENDENT OBSERVERS

Social Self-Confidence
(3.2)

1	2	3	4	5	6	7
Panicky in social situations. Makes excuses for self. Shrinks from making new adjustments.		Is assured with friends and in accustomed situations. Capable of adjusting to new situations requiring poise and confidence.			Very assured social behavior with both adults and children. Takes failure in matter-of-fact way. Invites new situations requiring poise and confidence.	

Popularity
(2.3)

1	2	3	4	5	6	7
Frequently avoided by others; his presence may be tolerated for short periods of time. Frequently left alone; socially isolated. (Is shunned, squeezed out of activities; ostracized.)		Generally accepted by others, or, popular with a small group. If conveniently situated, social contact may be made with him by anyone who happens to be present.			Generally approved and admired by others. Efforts repeatedly made by others to attract his attention. A preferred partner in activities; his company sought by many.	

[6] The sequence of rating schedules used in this study will be described in detail in other publications from the Institute of Child Welfare.

TABLE 2 (*Continued*)

Grooming Activity

(4.1)

1	2	3	4	5	6	7

Pays no attention to personal appearance. Can't be bothered about how appearance impresses others.	Offers evidence of some attention to clothes, hair, nails, shoes, etc.; but grooming not a major or very important activity.	Obviously spends a great deal of time in grooming self. Frequently arranges or combs hair, brushes off clothes.

Attractiveness of Appearance

(3.2)

1	2	3	4	5	6	7

Very unattractive; unattractive coloring and features; poor carriage, asymmetrical proportions; unpleasing expression; unkempt; ill-fitting, inappropriate clothes, excessively fat or thin.	Pleasing and attractive in some of the factors listed in "1."	Extremely attractive and pleasing appearance, including coloring, features, proportion of body, carriage, cleanliness, facial expression, becoming clothes, proper distribution of fat.

In describing the process by which John reached a somewhat more satisfying social rôle, we must keep in mind the complexity of the social organization with which he was confronted. Although our ratings and comments reveal substantial gains made by John during his last year in high school, it is clear that his progress in social relationships did not apply to the "inner" cliques of students who set the prestige pattern. An increasing number of his classmates seemed to welcome him as a group member, with an appreciation of his growing humor and informed intellectual interests, but his social index was still exactly zero with the "élite." John's relationships with girls were subject to similar limitations of status. Those who belonged or hoped to belong to the socially anointed groups were disposed to scorn or ignore him. Perhaps this was a natural outcome of the tendency sometimes noted, to classify boys as either (*a*) romantically eligible, or (*b*) utterly impossible,[7] and it would readily be conceded that John at this period was not a romantic figure. But among girls of his own less pretentious circle, he was beginning to be accepted with an easy and friendly rapport. One would expect these changes to result in an increased poise and self-confidence, and our records suggest that such was indeed the case. But there were also some continued indications of unadaptability to the behavior expected of him in social situations. There was still a certain inflexible insistence on his own demands and a tendency to be critical of others. And there was also from time to time an ambitious urge to join the activities of a larger group than that which accepted him.

The foregoing has included only a small fraction of the observational records about John. From these excerpts, and from the observational data as a whole, we conclude that during John's last year of high school a genuinely favorable trend was occurring in several aspects of his social behavior. He was showing some growth in companionability. He was making greater efforts to conform with the group in manners and skills. And he had won a more objective attitude toward his own problems. That problems still persisted is indicated by his uneasiness in any unfamiliar social situation; his continued tendency to incur scorn or ridicule, in some form, from many of his associates; and, in return, his occasional critical, censorial attitudes toward others. The major conflicts present since his elementary school days were by no means resolved, but as John set out to college there were many indications that he was learning to function acceptably in spite of these sources of disturbance.

---

[7] In the vernacular, "Smooth Guys" *vs.* "Drips."

When we look to the future, it is less easy to offer a prediction, on the basis of observational records, than in the case of boys who are more secure in their social relationship and in their internal resources. As expressed by one staff member,

John's most pressing needs include the opportunity for freedom of artistic and intellectual expression; congenial contacts among others who share his interests; and the supporting companionship of at least one good friend. With this favoring help, we may expect him to continue the positive trends already begun.

Chapter V

PHYSICAL DEVELOPMENT

A. HEALTH RECORD

John's lack of robust health was apparent to all who knew him. Not merely in the earlier grades but even in senior high school we find such comments as the following:

"John gets tired too easily—seems to have little physical reserve."

"John has been absent for two days; his mother reported that he stayed home to rest."

"During the fourth period, John has been so sleepy he could hardly keep his eyes open. Yawns frequently and long, puts his head on the desk. . . ."

"John is still having numerous colds. He looks fatigued—feels tired if he doesn't get to bed by 8:30."

Such marked physical limitations, whatever their origin, could hardly fail to have some effect upon his school work. During the first four terms of elementary school, he was absent more than half of the time. After the sixth grade his attendance record was fair, averaging only two or three absences a month, but his physical vigor was frequently unequal to the demands of a full day's work. This may account in part for the occasional reports from teachers who were impressed by the fact that his achievement was irregular and seemed to fall below expectation. Although these teachers were undoubtedly aware of John's frail health, a sympathetic understanding was sometimes difficult in the face of his asthenic querulousness, his failure to muster any of the admired qualities of robust and vigorous response to the world about him. If the traits accompanying his lack of vitality were to some extent a social handicap with his teachers they were of course even more so with his classmates. In an adolescent culture which values "pep," the "snappy comeback," and the dynamic scintillation of the "go-getter," John's sober restraint and physical weakness could hardly lead to popularity. Only through some other favorable traits, strongly compensating for these physical deficiencies, could he expect to win status among teen-age associates; in preceding sections, however, we have seen that John was quite generally lacking in characteristics possessing a social appeal. He was caught in a vicious circle: unfavorable traits led to rejection in the very field in which he had strong aspirations (social acceptance); and this rejection, through its emotional consequences, had a further depressant effect upon his general well-being.

The usual childhood illnesses are noted in the school medical record, including a severe case of measles; bronchitis, otitis, and repeated minor upsets—indigestion, constipation, colds. This record of "delicate" health persisted into adolescence, with minor digestive upsets, an under-nourished condition, and marked susceptibility to colds. From the age of 11.5 years, John received a physical examination at the Institute at approximately six-month intervals until the age of 18.5. In the first examination, the physicians noted little in the way of physical handicaps, with the exception of a muscular development slightly below normal. At 12.5, however, they recorded him as relatively immature; his dental development was definitely below average, and no increase in testicular growth had been noted as yet. He showed a tendency toward a feminine distribution of fat, retarded pubic-hair development, and small genitals. This retardation in sexual development, so obvious to the physicians, was by other signs also apparent to his classmates, who at this age were beginning to accord a special measure of prestige to indications of masculinity and of growing up.

B. PHYSICAL GROWTH

At the time of the first anthropometric measurements (age 11.4 years) John weighed approximately 80 lbs. and stood slightly over 4 ft. 9 in. in height. Seen on the playground among his classmates he appeared approximately average in physical size and conformation. But in the following years John grew more slowly than his classmates. He lagged behind in height, in weight, in nearly every measure of physical size. With the tediously slow increments characteristic of delayed maturing (85 per cent of the boys in his group were earlier in maturity than John) he dropped to the twenty-fifth percentile in height, the fifteenth percentile in weight, below the tenth percentile in shoulder breadth. This was in the high-ninth grade, age 15, his lowest point in physical status relative to the group, and also (if the reader will recall) an exceptionally bad period in nearly every measure of social relationships as observed by his classmates and by adults.

Figure 6 presents, in silhouette form,[1] seriatim annual photographs for John. This illustration gives a clear indica-tion of John's somewhat narrow body build, persisting into maturity; his gradual growth from 12 to 15 years; and a sudden spurt in growth from 15 to 16. Figure 7 illustrates growth in height as related to his age-mates. In the preparation of this chart, the average for boys in the Adolescent

---

[1] As a part of the program of physical studies, conducted by Dr. H. R. Stolz, body photographs, nude, were taken under standard conditions at each semiannual physical examination. For the present purpose, photographs are included only for year intervals; the effect shown in the published plate was obtained by taking a contact print of a paper positive, with over-exposure to eliminate details which would reveal personal identity.

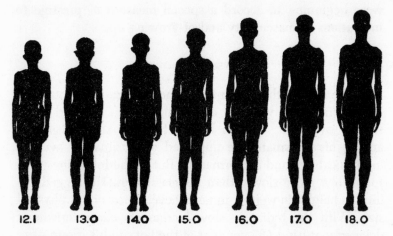

12.1   13.0   14.0   15.0   16.0   17.0   18.0

FIG. 6.—SILHOUETTES FROM BODY PHOTOGRAPHS AT YEAR INTERVALS

Growth Study is represented by a smoothed solid line, the actual age means being shown as points on or adjacent to the line. The larger dots indicate the measurements obtained for John, at approximately six-month intervals. From 11.5 to 12.5 years of age, John is seen to be almost exactly average in height. From this point, however, he dropped progressively below the average, until at fourteen and a half he reached the lower margin of the shaded area which in this chart represents the middle 50 per cent of our cases (± 1 P.E. from the mean). John was, at this time, still a "little boy" among classmates the majority of whom were further advanced in the cycle of pubertal development toward adulthood. By every external indication he seemed destined to become an undersized adult. But within this year a change in growth rate occurred, leading to a belated growth spurt through which he eventually caught up with the average for his group.

Another way in which growth data can be presented, bringing into sharper relief the variation in rates at suc-

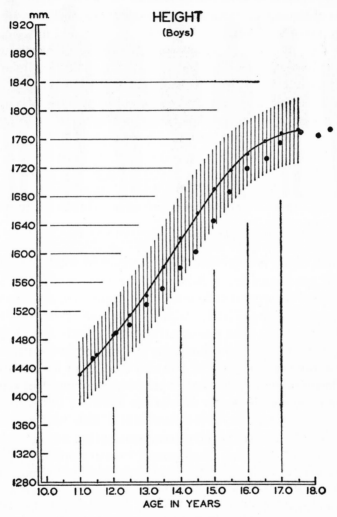

FIG. 7.—GROWTH CURVE FOR HEIGHT (BOYS)

cessive ages, is to show the *increments* according to specified units of time. A convenient unit to use is a decimal part of a year. Table 3 exhibits John's growth in height and in weight with computations of (*a*) absolute gains per .1 of a year and (*b*) percentage gains per year. It can be noted that John's greatest velocity of growth in height was after the age of 15 (that is, in the year period ending at 16 he grew 74 mm., or 7.4 mm. per .1 of a year). His growth in weight was less even and regular, but with the largest absolute gain also falling in the sixteenth year.

TABLE 3

JOHN'S GROWTH IN HEIGHT AND WEIGHT FROM AGE 12.1 TO 18.1

Age	Height			Weight		
	Mm.	Increment per .1 Year	% Gain per Year	Kg.	Increment per .1 Year	% Gain per Year
12.1	1489 *			38.0		
13.0	1529	4.4	3.0	38.6	.7	1.8
14.0	1580	5.1	3.3	43.9	5.3	13.7
15.0	1644	6.4	4.1	47.4	3.5	8.0
16.0	1718	7.4	4.5	53.5	6.1	12.9
17.0	1753	3.5	2.0	55.5	2.0	3.7
18.1	1765	1.1	.7	60.0	4.1	7.4

* In terms of feet and inches, John's height at 12.1 years was 4′ 10½″; at 18.1 years, 5′ 9½″. His weight at 12.1 was 84 lbs., at 18.1, 132 lbs.

C. SKELETAL MATURING

To the superficial observer (and also to John himself) his growth record during this adolescent period was exceptional almost to the point of abnormality. It had serious consequences in his ability to hold his own with his peers—an ability already compromised, as we have seen, by other deficiencies. And yet in terms of more fundamental characteristics, John's growth in height was entirely normal. This

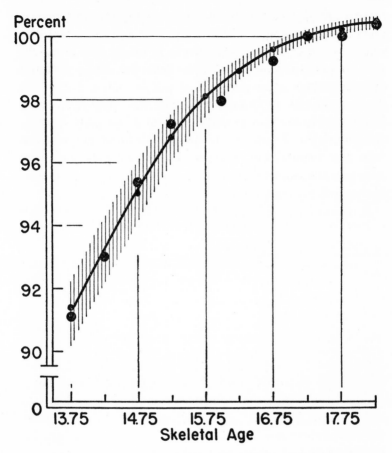

FIG. 8.—RELATIVE GROWTH IN HEIGHT, ACCORDING TO PHYSIOLOGICAL AGE

is illustrated in Figure 8, which shows his *relative* growth, the percentage of mature height,[2] presented according to his physiological rather than his chronological age. Physiological age, in this instance, is determined through X-rays of the

---

[2] Mature height is taken as the height reached at 17.6 years. At this time his skeletal maturity was sufficiently complete so that further growth in height could be expected to be negligible.

hand and knee, evaluated with reference to the Todd standards for skeletal maturing.[3] In this figure, the solid line
represents the average relative height of all of the boys in
the sample, classified according to their physiological (skeletal) ages. The points representing John's relative height, are
close to the line of the averages, showing that in terms of
basic maturation his growth in height is normal and consistent. Although apparently grossly retarded in height at
14 and 15 years of age, his skeletal maturity indices at those
ages make possible the prediction that his ultimate mature
height will be approximately average for his group.

In growth patterns of the type illustrated here, we note
the possibility of a complete physical recovery from a period
marked by deviate physical characteristics. It is not always
as easy, however, to recover from the psychological consequences of a growth record which, in the adolescent period,
fails to conform to group norms and group expectations.

D. GROWTH CURVES RELATIVE TO THE GROUP

Since our interest in the details of John's physical growth
is primarily from the point of view of possible social impli-
cations, it will be useful to consider another type of growth
curve in which each measure is expressed in terms of standard scores comparable to those previously shown for psychological traits (Chapters III and IV).

Figure 9 presents these relative growth curves for a selection of three measurements: height, stem length,[4] and bi-iliac

---

[3] The technique of X-ray assessment has been described by N. Bayley,
"Skeletal X-rays as Indicators of Maturity," *Journal of Consulting Psychology*,
Vol. 4, 1940, pp. 69-73.

[4] Stem length involves the measurement of the length of the trunk and
head when the subject is sitting with his back against an upright measuring
board, and his upper legs are at a 45° angle with the floor. Bi-iliac width is
a measure of hip width; it is recorded from sliding calipers, the jaws of
which are placed firmly at the iliac crests.

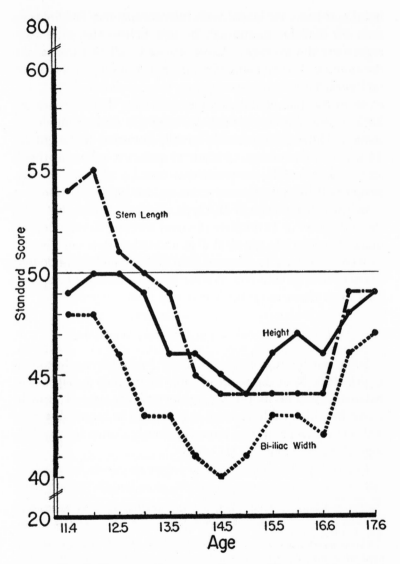

FIG. 9.—STANDARD SCORES FOR PHYSICAL MEASUREMENTS
Stem length, Height, Bi-iliac width

width. In the case of each of these components of physique
we note that the seriatim measurements begin near the average, recede to a lower position, and then return to the
average. This is a characteristic picture of a late maturing
individual.

In other measurements John showed a similar tendency
to lag behind the average after age 12. Unfortunately, in
some of these physical traits he failed to recover the ground
lost in the early teens. Figure 10 presents relative growth
curves for weight, arm circumference, and chest circumference. In these curves a more or less stable position was
reached around the age of 15; this does not mean that John
ceased growing in these characteristics, but merely that he
failed to show an *accelerated* growth to compensate for the
earlier period of deceleration. Having dropped to the lowest
15 per cent of the group, in later years he remained approximately in the same relative status.

Thus in John's case we see an illustration of the fact that
the physical growth of an individual has an individual pattern, not merely with regard to the timing of changes in the
rate of growth, but also with regard to the relationship of
parts. This relationship, in the case of John, is one in which
his mature physique is characterized by a normal height and
a fairly normal development of the abdominal trunk and
legs, but a weak and fragile development of the upper part
of the body comprising the arms, shoulder girdle, and chest.
This can also be seen in a study of the silhouettes in figure 6.
In John's physique, and more basically, we may infer, in
his endocrine organization, occur parallels to our records of
his interests, attitudes and activities, which were often characterized as differing from those of his more vigorously masculine classmates.[5]

---

[5] Various investigators have attempted to provide a systematic basis for the
classification of body proportions. The most recent work in this field (W. H.

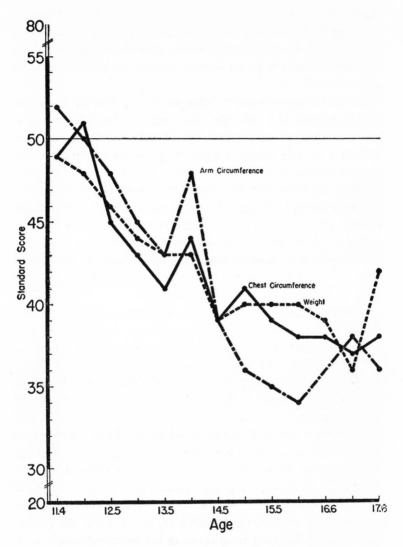

FIG. 10.—STANDARD SCORES FOR PHYSICAL MEASUREMENTS
Arm circumference, Chest circumference, Weight

E. PHYSIOLOGICAL CHANGES

The basal metabolism or basal oxygen consumption of an individual indicates the energy requirements needed to maintain the normal vital processes when activity is reduced to a minimum. Clinically it has been found that this basal energy requirement is closely associated with the functional activity of the thyroid gland; when the thyroid gland is underactive, the basal metabolism is reduced. Except at the clinical extremes, the psychological factors associated with high or low metabolism have not been clearly established, but in a comprehensive study of the individual a knowledge of this aspect of bodily function is sometimes of value.

The following table (4) shows the cumulative measurements of John's basal metabolism, and also averages for a

Sheldon, S. S. Stevens, and W. B. Tucker, *The Varieties of Human Physique* (New York, Harper, 1940), xii, 347 pp., has dealt with three principal components of physical constitution, the "endomorphic," "mesomorphic," and "ectomorphic," defined as follows:

"Endomorphy means relative predominance of soft roundness throughout the various regions of the body.... Mesomorphy means relative predominance of muscle, bone and connective tissue. The mesomorphic physique is normally heavy, hard and rectangular in outline.... Ectomorphy means relative predominance of linearity and fragility. In proportion to his mass, the ectomorph has the greatest surface area and hence relatively the greatest sensory exposure to the outside world. Relative to his mass he also has the largest brain and central nervous system."

For any given individual, each of these components can be classified on a 7-point scale. In *endomorphy* John Sanders in his later adolescence falls slightly below the midpoint of this scale. In *mesomorphy* he is markedly below, and in *ectomorphy* definitely above the middle of the scale.

In individuals of this general make-up, however, a precise classification is often difficult because of dysplasias (differing proportion of the components in different parts of the body). John's physique is marked by such disharmony. In the region of the head and neck his classification is "3-2-5" (referring again to the 7-point scale for each of the three components). In the region of the chest he is nearer normal in the endomorphic component, with a classification of "4-2-5." In the region of the trunk he becomes "4-3-5," and is nearest the middle of the scale in the region of the legs, with a classification of "4-3-4"; here, with his poorly developed muscles, he deviates from a middle value of 4 only in the mesomorphic component.

group of approximately fifty boys in the study, in terms of physical units (calories per square meter per hour [6]) and in terms of the percentage deviation from the Boothby-Sandiford norms.[7] Each measurement is based on six determinations, made on two successive days.

TABLE 4

COMPARISON OF JOHN'S BASAL METABOLISM BETWEEN AGES 12.5 AND 18.0 WITH THAT OF FIFTY OTHER BOYS OF THE SAME AGES

Age	Calories per Square Meter per Hour		% Deviation B.M.R.	
	J.S.	Mean of Group	J.S.	Mean of Group
12.5	43.0	44.4 ± .38	− 9.4	− 6.1
13.1	40.8	44.1 ± .30	− 13.2	− 6.1
13.4	40.6	43.2 ± .36	− 13.7	− 7.1
14.1	39.1	43.5 ± .35	− 14.9	− 5.5
14.6	37.4	42.9 ± .32	− 17.9	− 5.9
15.1	43.6	42.8 ± .35	− 3.2	− 5.2
15.5	42.7	41.4 ± .38	− 4.1	− 6.7
16.0	39.8	41.1 ± .38	− 9.6	− 6.7
17.0	38.0	41.0 ± .47	− 12.7	− 6.5
18.0	38.0	————	− 10.7	——

For the earlier part of John's record (age 12.5 to 14.6, low seventh to low ninth grade), the most striking fact to be noted is the relatively low basal metabolic rate. Since the

---

[6] In connection with the present study, it was found that the most reliable expression of basal metabolism is in terms of heat production, in calories, per unit of surface of the body. Calories are indirectly determined by the Tissot open-circuit gasometer method, in which the total expired air is collected for a measured time interval, its volume is measured, and the concentration of oxygen and CO_2 is determined. The surface area of the body, in square meters, is calculated from height and weight by the Du Bois formula; see N. W. Shock, "Standard Values for Basal Oxygen Consumption in Adolescence," *American Journal of Diseases of Children,* Vol. 64, 1942, pp. 19-32.

[7] W. M. Boothby and I. Sandiford, "Normal Values of Basal or Standard Metabolism. A Modification of the Du Bois Standards," *American Journal of Physiology,* Vol. 90, 1929, pp. 290-291.

mean B.M.R. for our cases is about 6 per cent below the average values for Minnesota children, as recorded by Boothby and Sandiford, John's record is less extreme than would at first appear, but he was nevertheless somewhat lower in B.M.R. than the majority of his classmates. Moreover, during this period he exhibited a definite *downward* trend, as compared with the norm. It will be recalled that this junior-high-school period was also, for John, marked by a downward trend in a number of aspects of social and psychological adjustment. It would not be wise to contend that a declining basal metabolism was the *cause* of a decline in other traits, particularly since the metabolic changes were so small in degree. These changes carry some weight, however, when considered as a part of a total developmental picture. The data on B.M.R. for these early years are in conformity with what we know about John's listlessness, his tendency to fatigue easily, and his generally low energy level.

At the age of 15 and 15.5 a new factor became apparent in connection with adolescent maturing. This was the time, as we have seen, of most rapid growth increments. Sexual maturing was also indicated by a more rapid genital development.[8] The growth of pubic hair had become accentuated shortly before the age of 15, and by age 16 was nearly complete.[9] Rises in basal metabolism are not uncommon during or shortly before the period of most rapid pubertal changes.

---

[8] Increase in rate of growth of the male organ was noted by the physicians as beginning at 14, and as being completed at 16. An earlier index of pubertal change is usually to be noted in an increased growth of the testicles; in the present case this occurred at about 12.5 years, and coincides roughly with the beginning of a pubertal cycle which reached a maximum expression at about 15 to 15.5 years, and which was concluded at about 18 years. For the group as a whole, the corresponding ages average about a year earlier.

[9] On the Davenport Scale, on which adult status is indicated by a rating of 6, the rating was 2 at the age of 14.5; 4 at the age of 15 and 5 at the age of 16.

In John's case this increase was very marked, and was accompanied by a number of other symptoms of heightened physiological activity. In circulatory functions, for example (systolic blood pressure, pulse pressure and pulse rate, observed under basal conditions), John in his early teens was characteristically below the group average. At the age of 15 this lag was no longer present; perhaps we can regard these multiple changes as an illustration of the pervasive way in which adolescent maturing is expressed in the organism.[10]

Attention may be called to one additional measure of physiological function, of particular interest to the student of psychosomatic relationships. Studies of hospital patients have indicated an association between anxiety states and an increase (beyond normal) in the amount of air breathed out.[11] It has also been shown that certain physical symptoms which such patients report may have their basis in the physiological upset produced by excessive breathing (hyperventilation). As measured under resting conditions, John's

---

[10] Another measure of maturing, in terms of a physiological function, is the amount of *creatine* observed in chemical analysis of the urine. Creatine is normally excreted in the urine of immature males. Sexual maturity brings an increased ability to utilize or otherwise dispose of creatine, so that it is no longer excreted into the urine. In the case of John Sanders, a fairly normal physiological adjustment was shown between 15.5 and 16 years, with a fall in creatine excretion. This adjustment, however, was not maintained, and for the following two years more creatine was excreted as he grew older. A change in this direction, quite atypical in boys at so late an age in adolescence, is perhaps a delayed expression of irregularities in the development of masculine traits. It was also associated, in John's case, with a period of lowered organic efficiency as judged from tests of pulse rate and breathing, after exercise. See N. W. Shock, *A Study of Creatine and Creatinine Excretion in Children* (in press).

[11] William J. Kerr, J. W. Dalton, and Paul A. Gliebe, "Some Physical Phenomena Associated with Anxiety States and Their Relation to Hyperventilation," *Annals of Internal Medicine*, Vol. 11 (December, 1937), pp. 961-992; Mayo H. Soley and N. W. Shock, "The Etiology of Effort Syndrome," *American Journal of Medical Sciences*, Vol. 196 (December, 1938), pp. 840-851; William J. Kerr, and others, "The Treatment of the Anxiety States," *Journal of the American Medical Association*, Vol. 113 (August, 1939), pp. 637-640.

respiratory volume [12] was characteristically low, at about the fifteenth percentile for the group of boys included in our sample for physiological measurements.

Even allowing for his slimness of build, John's vital capacity [13] was small. After the age of 14, however, measurements under resting conditions showed a sharp increase in respiratory volume, owing to the development of exceptionally rapid although shallow breathing.[14] Three years later in the high eleventh grade, a similar tendency was shown in our records, although to a smaller degree. When we compare these physiological changes with records of psychological trends, as noted in other sections, a general correspondence, not too exact, can be seen between periods of "hyperventilation" (as marked by rapid and shallow breathing) and periods involving intensified anxiety and emotional reactions to loss of social status. The high point in respiratory rate, in his fifteenth year, is a period marked by declining indexes in many aspects of adjustment.

---

[12] Liters of air per square meter of body surface per minute.

[13] Vital capacity is the maximum amount of air that can be expired from the lungs after a maximum (voluntary) inspiration.

[14] The change in rate was from 16.3 per minute at age 14, to 20.7 per minute at age 14.5, as compared with a group average, under resting conditions, of about 16. Based on repeated measurements on two days, these records reflect a functional change of some magnitude, and not merely a transient response. At the same time a marked reduction occurred in tidal volume, signifying shallow breathing or a small volume of air per breath, in relation to the surface area of the body. While we cannot be certain that his respiratory symptoms were an expression of emotional disturbances, no other interpretation seems equally probable. This would, then, be a further link in a sequence of psychosomatic relationships; we have seen that John's inadequacies in health and general physique were in part a source of his emotional difficulties. If these, in turn, were sufficiently profound to bring about the degree of overbreathing which has been recorded, we might expect a still further step in the cumulative chain of circumstance; the changes in John's breathing functions were sufficiently great so that they could not be long continued without some temporary ill effects upon other aspects of health and physical efficiency. In the physician's record at age 14.5, it is not surprising to find the notation, "Boy does not seem well—a generally below par condition."

Chapter VI

MOTOR AND MENTAL ABILITIES

The boy who is conspicuously undersized during the early part of the pubertal cycle is sometimes known to others as "an active small boy." The social recognition that he wins through sheer physical activity may compensate, in a measure, for traits in which he is lacking. We have seen, however, that John was both slow in maturing and deficient in juvenile energies. He possessed no athletic interests [1] which could help him to maintain status among his classmates. Nor was his muscular development adequate to the demands of the playground, in competition with more rapidly developing associates. This can be seen not merely in the physicians' records ("this boy is poor in muscle tone, and with muscular development below his age level"), but also in the repeated records of manual strength based on measurements with a hand dynamometer.

A. STRENGTH RECORD

Table 5 gives the obtained strength measurements for John (left hand as well as right hand) and the means for boys and girls in the study.[2] With considerable uniformity, the mean left-hand strength of the (right-handed) boys was about 93 per cent of the right-hand strength. John, with sub-

---

[1] Chapter VII, *infra*.

[2] For the earlier measurements approximately ninety boys and ninety girls are included; the numbers drop to seventy-eight boys and seventy-two girls at seventeen years.

jective preference for the right hand, was exceptional in showing a slightly stronger grip with the non-preferred than with the preferred hand.[3] In view of the frequent reports of feminine tendencies in physical characteristics and behavior, it is interesting to note that his general strength record was more similar to that of girls than of boys; he was, in fact, below the girls' average during the earlier half of the study.

TABLE 5

LEFT- AND RIGHT-HAND STRENGTH OF JOHN FROM AGE 11.5 TO 17.5, COMPARED WITH THAT OF OTHER BOYS AND GIRLS OF THE SAME AGES

	Grip Right Hand (in Kg.)			Grip Left Hand (in Kg.)		
Age	Mean for Boys	Mean for Girls	J.S.	Mean for Boys	Mean for Girls	J.S.
11.5 *	26.3	22.6	18.0	24.9	20.2	20.0
12.0	27.6	24.2	20.0	26.3	21.4	21.0
12.5	29.4	26.4	18.0	27.7	23.5	20.5
13.0	31.0	27.7	23.0	28.8	24.0	22.0
13.5	33.4	28.7	20.0	31.5	25.9	23.0
14.0	36.3	29.2	28.5	33.8	26.4	28.5
14.5	39.5	30.3	22.5	37.1	27.1	24.0
15.0	43.4	32.5	30.5	40.5	28.3	28.0
15.5	46.6	33.1	31.0	43.6	29.8	32.0
16.0	49.1	33.7	30.5	45.6	30.8	33.5
16.5	51.7	34.6	37.0	48.7	31.4	40.5
17.0	54.5	35.2	40.0	50.1	31.8	40.5
17.5	56.3	35.8	37.0	52.3	31.8	38.0

* The figure given is the midpoint of the class interval; thus the 11.5 age group includes all cases from 11.25 to 11.74 years. John's age at each testing was within .1 of a year of this midpoint.

In an additional dynamometer test involving strength of thrust, John's performance was approximately at the tenth

[3] Tests of the sighting eye showed that John was a "crossed dextral" (left-eyed, right-handed). His right hand, however, was more skilled than the left; in tests of eye-hand coördination his dextrality index (right-hand score divided by left-hand score) was approximately as high as the average.

percentile until the age of 16, and then fell even lower, relative to the group. In a test of strength of pull his record was somewhat better, moving up to the twenty-fifth percentile at age 17.[4]

B. PHYSICAL ABILITIES

When John was in the high eighth grade a series of playground tests of physical abilities was administered to the members of the study, with repetitions in later semesters until the low twelfth grade. The test included two track events given under standardized conditions (50 Yard Dash, Broad Jump); the Jump and Reach test (distance between the highest point that can be touched, and the highest point that can be reached in jumping); the Distance Throw of a playground baseball; and the Brace Tests (a series of twenty tests of body balance and coördination).[5]

At 14 years, John could throw a baseball one-third as far as the average boy of his age (43′ as compared with 121′). He could jump half as high as the average (6″ as compared with 12½″). His best broad jump was 4′ 3″ as compared with the boys' average of 6′ 3″ at the same age. For the most part, John's scores in successive years ranged from the fifth to the fifteenth percentile and only in a few instances moved above the twenty-fifth percentile. No definite trends were noted, except that (in conformity with other physical records) he was at his worst in his fifteenth year and improved in the

---

[4] The Thrust and Pull tests (sometimes called Chest Push and Chest Pull) register the strength of the shoulder extensors and retractors. Chest Push is measured with the dynamometer resting on the sternum; the subject pushes inward with the two hands, trying to "crush" the apparatus. In the Chest Pull the dynamometer is in the same position, but the subject pulls outward, trying to "tear it apart."

[5] The tests and the group results have been described in the following monograph: A. Espenschade, "Motor Performance in Adolescence," *Monographs of the Society for Research in Child Development,* Vol. 5, No. 1 (1940), 126 pp.

year following. In the broad jump, for example, he made a sudden gain from 4′ 7″ at 15 years, to 6′ 6″ at 15.5 years. In the Jump and Reach test a similar sharp improvement was shown, from 7½″ at 15 to 12½″ at 15.5. These gains were due chiefly to an improved musculature in the legs, and were paralleled by an increased leg and thigh circumference. The upper part of the body, as we have seen in Chapter V, failed to show an equally favorable development, and the continued physical retardation in shoulder breadth and arm circumference found expression in continued poor records for manual and arm strength and for throwing a ball.

Figure 11 presents the average for our group of boys on the Brace Test, with a shaded area extending to 1 S.D. below the mean. Approximately only the poorest 15 per cent of the cases fall below this shaded area. John's own growth curve is indicated by a broken line. In his first testing, at age 14, he was far below the group average, but later succeeded in coming closer to a normal performance.

Figure 12 presents comparative scores, before and after sexual maturing, for all of the physical ability tests, and also for the average of four strength tests (right- and left-hand grip, thrust, and pull). In this figure, the solid line presents a profile of John's performance based on an average for two tests given in the last year of junior high school. The broken line represents the profile for the average of the same tests given in the high eleventh and low twelfth grades. Gains, relative to the group mean at 50, are indicated by the cross-hatched area.[6] Even after physiological maturing resulted in some degree of improvement in John's physical abilities, he was still so inferior to the group as a whole that this remained a factor of some importance in his social relationships and in

---

[6] As in other figures, the standard scores are computed with the group mean at 50, and with 10 points equalling one standard deviation. In this case, however, reference is to a grade group rather than an age group.

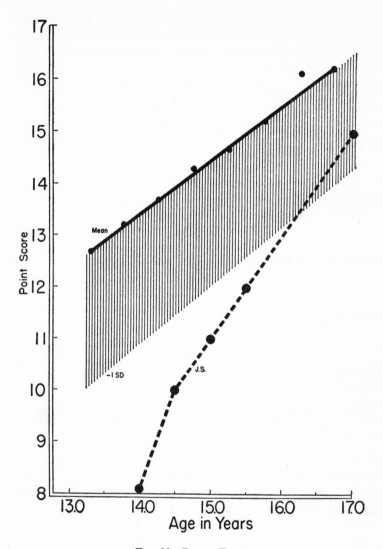

Fig. 11.—Brace Test

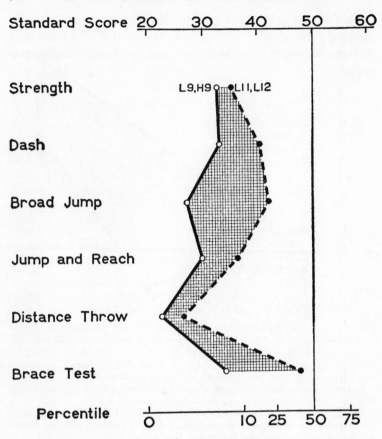

FIG. 12.—PHYSICAL ABILITY PROFILE

his feelings of personal adequacy. The rôle played by this physical-inferiority factor (or group of factors) will be more fully discussed in Chapter X.

C. MANUAL ABILITIES

In addition to the tests of strength and gross motor function described above, the Adolescent Growth Study included in its program a number of tests of fine motor function, beginning with simple reaction time to a sound, and extending through a variety of serial action and eye-hand coördination tests.[7]

TABLE 6

STANDARD SCORES FOR MANUAL ABILITIES

Reaction Time
    Right Hand 48.8
    Left Hand 49.6
Bimanual Coördination 49.8
Manual Steadiness 49.8
Rotary Speed
    Right Hand 47.6
    Left Hand 48.7
Serial Action
    Right Hand 45.1
    Left Hand 44.1
Serial Discrimination 35.4
Rhythmic Eye-Hand Coördination... 29.9

Table 6 presents standard scores for John's performance in these tests. Since the cumulative records for John showed no

---

[7] Descriptions of these tests follow:

Simple reaction time: Time of response to an auditory signal, measured by Cenco counter on a modified form of the Miles reaction board.

Bimanual Coördination; Using two hands simultaneously in packing spools in a tray (a modified form of the Brown spool packer).

Manual Steadiness: The Seashore Steadiness Test: a metal stylus is thrust into an aperture at a speed determined by a metronome. Apertures are of decreasing size in successive trials.

Rotary Speed: The Miles Speed Drill, with electric counter attached. The handle of the drill is rotated, with wrist movement.

Serial Action: Serial placement of a stylus on the Miles reaction board.

Rhythmic Eye-hand Coördination: The Jones Synchrometer; steel balls are electromagnetically released from a chute into a revolving slot.

Serial Discrimination: The Serial Discrimeter, from the Stanford Motor Skills Unit. The subject responds to a number which appears in a window of the apparatus, by depressing a lever similarly numbered.

Procedures and group results for Reaction Time have been described by H. E. Jones, "Reaction Time and Motor Development," *American Journal of Psychology*, Vol. 50, 1937, pp. 181-194. Several of the other tests are described by R. H. Seashore, "Individual Differences in Motor Skills," *Journal of Genetic Psychology*, Vol. 3, 1930, pp. 38-66.

definite trends in standard scores during the period of the study, the values given are averages for all administrations of the tests between the ages of 11.4 and 16. Three administrations are involved for the Drill Speed Test, four for the Steadiness Test, and five for each of the others. Group averages approached growth limits in these functions before 16.

In the simpler speed tests (Reaction Time, Rotary Speed) John's scores were on the average almost exactly at the group mean. He was also close to the mean in the Manual Steadiness test, and in a simple Bimanual Coördination test. On more complex tasks, requiring concentration on a series of precise motor adjustments, his record was less satisfactory. In four tests out of five he fell below the average in Serial Action (a task requiring speed and accuracy in serial placement of a metal stylus); his average was at the thirty percentile. He was consistently poor, averaging in the lowest 10 per cent, in Serial Discrimination (a task involving selective finger action in depressing keys designated by a visual number series). Finally, his average was in the poorest 5 per cent in another serial test requiring manual coördination to visual cues (the Synchrometer Test). His persistent ineptness in this latter function is perhaps attributable to a factor which we have noted as a special handicap to John in other types of tests: the *rate* at which he was forced to work was externally determined, whereas he, himself, set the rate of response in the coördination tests in which he was closer to the average. While his manual and perceptuo-manual abilities were on the whole somewhat superior to those shown on motor tests involving muscular strength, general bodily coördination and athletic proficiency, it is apparent that John possessed no outstanding skill in any simple motor function involving speed or precision. "Often average, never superior," is the general characteristic of his performance in this field.

D. MENTAL ABILITIES

John's mediocre school record (Chapter III) seems inappropriate when we consider his consistent and genuine intellectual interests. If the latter are an indication of exceptional intelligence, we should have grounds for believing that his difficulties in school were due to lack of motivation, and that the school had somehow failed in offering any effective challenge to his efforts. In John's case, however, a poor-to-average assortment of school grades was fairly well matched by his performance in standard tests.

On his first intelligence test [8] at age 9 he attained an IQ of 98. A second test [9] at age 12 yielded an IQ of 101. These measures, however, may have underestimated John's abilities to some extent. He was not at his best in a group test situation requiring him to work under pressure. This was illustrated in results from the C A V D [10] test, which was given in the low sixth grade as a two-hour "speed test." Age norms are lacking to permit determination of an IQ, but his performance was one-half standard deviation below the average of his group (standard score 45.6). A year later the same test was administered as a "power" test, with unlimited time; John's score, in terms of C A V D levels of ability, rose approximately one standard deviation to a scale value of 56.1. This discrepancy suggests one possible reason for John's difficulties in classes demanding a minutely scheduled efficiency. His abilities were mustered slowly, and sometimes failed to stand up under effort.

It is instructive to consider, in Table 7, the series of IQ's obtained in standard tests given between the ages of 12 and

---

[8] The Detroit Primary Intelligence Test, given by the school in the third grade.

[9] Kuhlmann-Anderson.

[10] E. L. Thorndike and others, *The Measurement of Intelligence* (New York, Teachers College, Columbia University, 1927), xxvi, 616 pp.

15. The range of scores, from 91 to 119, while greater than would be usually found, is evidence of the danger of basing judgments on single tests. The most reliable measures are those based on the last three administrations of the Terman Group Test.[11] The question may be raised, however, as to whether these IQ's have not been aided by the amount of practice received. Since our chief interest is in comparing John with his classmates, we can eliminate the effects of repeated testing by computing standard scores based on the performance of the total group, all of whom received the same schedule of tests. When this is done, we find John's scores ranging about the average, from a standard score of 43 to one of 56.

TABLE 7

INTELLIGENCE TESTS: CUMULATIVE RECORD

Test	C.A.	I.Q.
Kuhlmann-Anderson	12.1	101
Terman Group Test A	12.6	119
Terman Group Test B	12.7	100
Stanford-Binet (1917 revision)	12.8	109
Kuhlmann-Anderson	14.1	91
Terman Group Test A	14.5	113
Terman Group Test B	14.6	112
Terman Group Test B	15.1	115

Do these variations show a systematic trend? Do they, like the cumulative results already reported for various physical, physiological and behavioral characteristics, relate themselves to other variables, such as age, health, sexual maturing, personal adjustment, or to changes in the educational or social environment? It is obvious that no such trends can be discerned. The IQ changes in Table 7 are partly a matter of

[11] For the total group the reliability of a single form of the Terman Group Test was .93.

differences in the tests, and partly due to personal and other factors contributing to unreliability of the tests.

There is no evidence that John's various handicaps, or his later partial conquest of these handicaps, exerted any appreciable net effect upon the development of his basic mental abilities. This is not in the least surprising, in view of studies of physical-mental relations [12] which have shown (in general, and within a normal range) that mental growth is relatively insensitive to perturbations in other areas of development. There is, however, evidence that John's intellectual functioning reflected his personality traits in characteristic ways. This is illustrated in the examiner's comments concerning his first Stanford-Binet test at the age of 12.7 years:

John showed a lively intellectual curiosity and was interested in a variety of things, but within each of these interests his attention seemed to be rigid and single-tracked. This lack of flexibility made it difficult for him to adapt to requirements when on unfamiliar ground. Upon encountering difficulties, he frequently demanded a pencil, because he could not "see" the words or numbers; I have never tested a more eye-minded person.

John's principal difficulties were on tests requiring precise operations, as in the use of numbers. With such tests he became insecure and often seemed confused, with slips of memory and errors in simple calculations. He asked to have instructions repeated, was dependent on the examiner, and easily discouraged. Although coöperative and anxious to do well, it was extremely hard for him to master a task (such as "memory span") in which he was required to be exact by fixed standards. If this is also true outside of the testing situation, it is not surprising that in his school work he has found great difficulty in learning to spell, in mastering the mechanics of English, and in learning a foreign language. We cannot tell from this test *why* he has had such unusual difficulty in this kind of learning. However, the supposition can be offered that in tasks involving an imaginative and analytic approach he imposes form upon himself; in tasks of the type which he

---

[12] N. W. Shock, and H. E. Jones, "Mental Development and Performance as Related to Physical and Physiological Factors," *Review of Educational Research*, Vol. 12, 1941, pp. 531-552.

finds difficult, form is imposed upon him from without. Resistance to such controls may account in part for the discrepancies between John's actual intelligence and his achievement in certain fields.

E. ACHIEVEMENT TESTS

John and his classmates took the Stanford Achievement Test four times during the period from the sixth through the ninth grade. For greater reliability, each annual administration involved the use of two forms of the test, at about a two-week interval.[13]

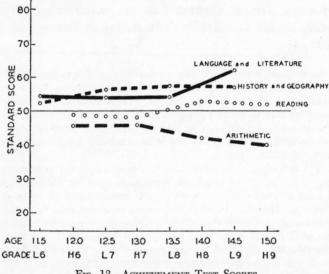

FIG. 13.—ACHIEVEMENT TEST SCORES

Results from eight subtests are presented in Table 8, in the form of educational quotients for specific subjects. The average of these educational quotients (107.6) is practically identical with the average intelligence quotient in Table 7

---

[13] In the sixth grade, the reliability of the combined forms, for boys, ranged from .83 (history and civics) to .96 (word meaning). In grade nine, reliabilities ranged from .92 to .96.

(107.5). Our chief attention, however, should be directed to the consistent differences in the results for different school subjects. These differences are shown graphically in Figure 13, which presents age curves based on standard scores; on the basis of content, the eight subtests have been combined into four pairs of tests. It can be seen that John's performance in "language and literature" was distinctly above the group average of 50. Consistent with his later interest in social studies were his superior scores (after the sixth grade) in "history and geography." John's scores in reading, fairly stable near the group average, were handicapped somewhat by his low reading speed.[14]

TABLE 8

EQ's in Specific Subjects

Age	11.8	12.1	12.4	13.1	13.5	14.1	14.8	15.1
Language Usage ..	117	——	115	——	115	——	117	——
Literature	121	——	118	——	112	——	113	——
History and Civics.	109	——	119	——	119	——	106	——
Geography	109	——	116	——	118	——	117	——
Reading (Paragraph Meaning)	——	114	——	106	——	117	——	111
Reading (Word Meaning)	——	105	——	107	——	110	——	108
Arithmetic Reasoning	——	106	——	100	——	88	——	82
Arithmetic Computation ...	——	100	——	90	——	82	——	87

[14] He was deliberate in this as in many other aspects of response. Photographic records of his eye movements during reading showed an exceptionally long "fixation pause," exceeded in length by only about 5 per cent of the class. He was also below average in visual acuity and in the ability to maintain binocular fusion. These latter factors are not necessarily correlated with reading ability, but together with refractive errors (astigmatism and farsightedness) they could be expected to produce discomfort in any type of close work, and (when uncorrected by glasses at a sufficiently early age) a tendency to avoid work involving precise visual adjustments. To no small degree, this may account for the early development of what John's teachers regarded as "careless" habits in various classroom routines.

Lower than the other curves and diverging from them is the cumulative curve for ability in arithmetic. As has often been found in other studies, the boys in this sample were on the average inferior to the girls in language usage and superior in arithmetic (particularly in arithmetic reasoning [15]). The general appearance of Figure 13, with the language curve above the group mean and the arithmetic curve below, is less typical for boys than for girls.

F. ASPECTS OF LEARNING ABILITY

Further clues concerning John's intellectual functioning can be found in the results from a series of experimental learning situations. These were of three general types: (a) learning involving motor trial and error, as in a stylus maze or punch-board,[16] (b) verbal learning by the method of paired associates [17] and (c) learning at a level involving inductive reasoning.[18] The regularity with which these tests were scheduled varied according to requirements of other parts of the program.

As shown in Table 9, John's performance in the first of these types of learning was fairly close to the average of the group, varying about the average. His scores in rational learning were also close to the average in the first two tests,

---

[15] W. A. Reynolds, *A Study of the Interrelationship of Measures of Achievement at Successive Grade Levels*. M. A. Thesis, University of California, 1941.

[16] For a description of apparatus and procedure in trial-and-error tests see H. E. Jones, and Joseph G. Yoshioka, "Differential Errors in Children's Learning on a Stylus Maze," *Journal of Comparative Psychology*, Vol. 25, 1938, pp. 463-480.

[17] H. D. Carter, H. E. Jones, and N. W. Shock, "An Experimental Study of Affective Factors in Learning," *Journal of Educational Psychology*, Vol. 25, 1934, pp. 203-215.

[18] The test of "rational" learning is described in F. T. Tyler, *Generalizing Ability of Junior High School Pupils: An Experimental Study of Rule Induction*. Ph.D. Dissertation, University of California, 1939.

TABLE 9

STANDARD SCORES IN LEARNING TESTS

Age	Trial and Error Learning	Rational Learning	Verbal Learning
12.0	—	48	—
12.5	—	—	33
13.0	47	51	48
13.5	44	—	41
14.0	47	—	20
14.5	51	40	36
15.0	48	—	44
15.5	—	44	35
16.0	58	—	45
16.5	47	—	44
17.0	—	—	—
17.5	—	45	—
Mean	48.8	45.6	38.4

but subsequently dropped to lower values. Perhaps this would be expected, in view of John's record in arithmetic reasoning. Although the inductive learning test does not require the use of numbers, for the group as a whole it is more closely related to arithmetic reasoning than to other variables. It is less to be expected that John would be as poor as he proved to be in learning verbal associations, especially in view of his language test scores and his interest in achievement at a verbal level. The results may, however, be related to what we know concerning his difficulty in adapting quickly to novel situations. In the analysis of the Stanford-Binet, we have noted John's tendency to be blocked or panicky on certain kinds of test items (such as tests of memory span), which are similar to laboratory situations in the element of "pressure" and in their strictly imposed criteria for success or failure. As a rule, John had relatively little difficulty with the trial-and-error experiments, perhaps because these involved problem-solving at a rate set by the subject himself. The verbal learning tests, however, were less congenial to his deliberate methods, due to their requirement of concentrated work at a rate externally imposed.

The varying efficiency shown by John in his reaction to different kinds of test material is probably related to genuine differences in his pattern of abilities. It is also likely that these differences are accentuated by personality factors which lie outside the realm of intellect, but which are consistently reflected in some aspects of intellectual functioning. This is, of course, by no means a unique finding. So far as practical considerations are concerned, such a condition would not necessarily weaken the validity of the tests; in the case of John it is apparent that somewhat the same restricting factors which operate in specific test situations are also revealed in his school work and in various aspects of everyday life.

Chapter VII

INTERESTS AND ATTITUDES

A. GROUP CHANGES

In the discussion of John's interests, it is well to keep in mind such demands as those set by his physical growth patterns, and his family situation, as well as those arising from the activities favored by his classmates. At the beginning of this study, boys and girls in the fifth and sixth grades had not completely relinquished their childhood. The boys were still, at times, playing with toy soldiers, marbles, mechano sets, electric trains. The girls were cutting out paper dolls and playing jacks. Both boys and girls roller-skated on the sidewalks, and coasted down hill in rackety wagons. John's most cherished possessions at this time were his "magic set," roller skates, and "bike." In addition to activities of this nature, the majority of the boys took part in such relatively mature activities as organized ball games on the school playground.

John seldom stayed after school to play with the other boys. His favorite pastimes were reading and drawing. Of all the group, he was the only one whose mother reported that he never played football or basketball, or similar active games of a less organized nature. Among John's classmates the devotion to games and sports lasted well into adolescence, although the time came when it had to share a place with interests in more definitely social boy-girl activities. An illustration of some of these group trends in interests is given

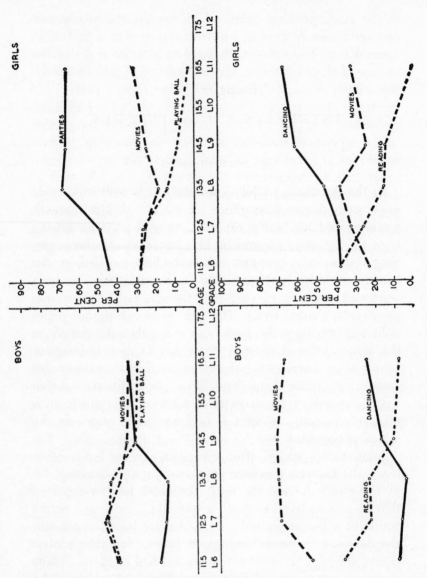

Fig. 14.—Choice of Things to Do

in the accompanying chart, which depicts the yearly percentage scores of boys and girls in response to a part of an interest test. The instructions were to indicate a preference for one of three activities. The first item in Figure 14, involving a comparison of "playing ball," "going to a party," and "going to the movies," shows that after the age of thirteen-and-a-half, boys report an increasing preference for parties, at the expense of the other two activities. The girls' interest in parties is greater at all ages, and shows an adolescent spurt that is characteristically earlier than in the case of boys. In the second item, comparing "dancing," "reading," and "going to the movies," boys and girls agree in their declining preference for reading, but disagree in the relative values assigned to dancing and movies. Many other examples could be given of specific interests which change with age, and which present different patterns among boys as compared with girls. John took the first of a series [1] of interest tests when he was in the low sixth grade, at the age of 11 years and 8 months. It can be said that he regarded the testing program seriously. From his year-to-year consistency in response, as well as from changes in response agreeing with other evidence of altered attitudes and behavior, we can assume that the answers given by John are, on the whole, an honest expression of his interests. On items that required selective checking, he was careful and discriminating. Frequently he furnished additional comment as to interests not

---

[1] Following is a list of the records drawn upon for the discussion of interests:

Name of Test	Times Given	Grades	Interval
U. C. Activity Record	10	8–12	6 months
U. C. Interest Record	7	6–12	12 "
Strong Vocational Interest Blank	3	10–12	12 "
Lehman and Witty Play Quiz	2	7–8	6 "

included in the check-list; such elaborate thoroughness was shown by few of his classmates, and indicated a rather high degree of conscientious effort. In the early records, however, his handwriting was nearly illegible and his spelling conformed to no recognized rules. In the sixth grade when John wrote that he would like to go to a "radio station," "station" was spell "stain." "Mugtion trick profer" was as far as he got without help when he wanted to indicate that he'd like to be a "magician,—a trick performer." His favorite actors were designated (in the low seventh grade) as "Loneol Baremore" and "Gerge O'Brian"; his favorite movie was "Washington Maskrade." He went to the movies in the seventh grade "vevery three moth." [2]

By the ninth grade, John had not changed his favorite actors. He had learned to spell George and now wrote "Loniel Barremore." In the tenth grade "Shurley temple" was so written. In the eleventh grade, Garbo's first name was "gretta"; even in the twelfth grade, John wrote "Rosline Russell," "Goldwin Follies," "Aulful Truth." His handwriting, which had improved steadily, was quite legible in the twelfth grade—perhaps equal to that of the average high school senior.

B. AREAS OF INTEREST

Figure 15 compares age curves for John's interests in four areas: intellectual-cultural; mechanical-scientific (M-S); social; and physical (interest in sports and physical activities). These curves are based on standard scores, comparable to those shown in preceding figures dealing with other

---

[2] Such responses suggest the difficulty of administering tests which require elementary, or even junior-high-school pupils, to do much writing. In this testing program an assistant checked over the papers in the classroom and at once returned incomplete papers so that help could be given in making responses more intelligible.

aspects of development.[3] Relative to his classmates, John's highest interest scores were on items classifiable as "intellectual," "esthetic," "cultural," "imaginative," "introspective,"

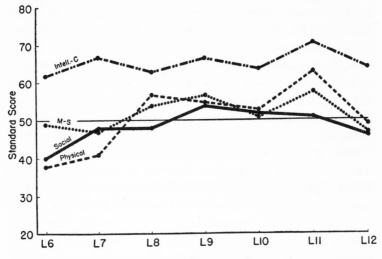

Fig. 15.—Standard Scores for Interests

and the like.[4] To these interests, moreover, he remained faithful at a time when they were sinking in value for his contemporaries; for the majority of John's classmates, intellectual and cultural interests and activities showed little

---

[3] The U. C. Interest Record, from which these scores were derived, was an adaptation and extension of the material included in earlier tests published by Symonds, Lehman and Witty, and Furfey. Approximately 400 items were selected with a view to sampling the interests of young people from the sixth grade in elementary school through high school. The material was classified to include "Things to Own," "Places to Go," "Magazines to Read," "Things to Be," and "Things to Do." Instructions were to respond to each item by indicating preference, indifference, or dislike.

[4] Contrary to the majority votes of his classmates, John showed persisting preferences for such items as "to be a writer"; "to keep a diary"; "to own a book of poems"; etc. In the eleventh and twelfth grades, 60 per cent of the boys voted that they would *not* want to "be a librarian"; John was among the 12 per cent who voted this as a desirable occupation.

gain during adolescence and often suffered a decline, in favor of more immediately social pursuits.

In the "mechanical" and "scientific" fields John never revealed special aptitudes; it does not surprise us that his interest scores, in this area, range irregularly about the group average of 50. He once indicated that he would be interested in "improving the beauty of a machine," but not in actually operating machines nor in studying theories of mechanical operations. In the Strong Vocational Interest Blank, which was given three times during senior high school, his occupational scores were uniformly low with regard to interests in science.

The age curve for John's social interests also varies about the mean, although our observational records (Chapter IV) indicate that John was considerably below the average in social participation. On our test blanks he frequently asserted a preference for such activities as "dancing," or "going to a party"; from other evidence, however, it has been apparent that this was a less intrinsic interest than, for example, his interest in reading. Perhaps we can infer that he desired to play a social rôle less for its own sake than for essentially personal reasons, associated with his need to feel more secure, to be recognized, and to believe in himself as a person. It may be noted, in Figure 15, that John's professed social interests were highest in the ninth grade, when his social capabilities were at their poorest (cf. Chapter IV).

In the sixth grade, John's lowest interest score was in the field of physical activities. As an eleven-year-old, the discrepancy between John's interests and those of his contemporaries is illustrated on every item involving athletics. The majority of his sixth grade classmates (89 per cent) indicated that they would like to own a football; 4 per cent were indifferent to this item, and 7 per cent were negative. John was among the indifferent ones. He was also, contrary to the majority, indifferent about owning a tennis racket, golf clubs, or a baseball and bat. With regard to actual participation, John tended to be negative rather than merely indifferent. Of John's classmates 75 per cent indicated that they would like to be on a school team; 14 per cent were indifferent, 12 per cent were negative. John was among the small minority casting a negative vote. Similarly, he indicated that he would not want to play football, that he would not want to play golf, and that he would not want to be an athletic coach (62 per cent of his classmates voted this as a desirable occupation).

It seems probable that John's early dislike for robust games like football and basketball was a consequence of poor health and physical inadequacy, as well as of his mother's desire to keep him safely at home. The prospect of entering into competition with boys in his class who were stronger and more skillful was not a pleasing one. In the eighth grade, however, there was evidence that John began to pay greater heed to the group values in regard to sports and to give them at least superficial acceptance. The interests that he now professed in this area were perhaps more "wishful" than realistic, since our activity records show that it was rare for him to take any actual part in playground games. This failure to play a normal rôle in physical activities can be more readily understood when we consider his physical development record (Chapter V). His *interest* in participating can also be understood as being based on social stirrings and personal dissatisfactions rather than on any real devotion to sports. The tensions created as a result of his differences from the group are suggested by his own later comments; in the senior year in high school he told his counsellor:

> The greatest mistake I ever made was not spending more time on the playgrounds. I should have been made to do it. Boys don't like you unless you can play games. It affects your whole personality.

C. MATURITY OF INTERESTS

Another group of activities on which John differed conspicuously from his classmates were those pertaining to juvenile play. Four of these activities are indicated in Figure

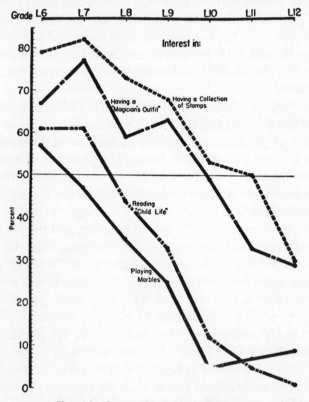

FIG. 16.—GROUP CHANGES IN INTERESTS

16, which shows the percentage of boys, in successive grades, reporting specified interests. The rapid decline in preference for these items during the early 'teens illustrates very clearly the "putting away of childish things" which is sometimes an almost ostentatious feature of adolescent maturing. John's response to such items, however, was usually on the side of continued preference rather than of adolescent rejection. After the ninth grade he deserted his earlier preference for reading *Child Life,* but as late as the eleventh grade remained firm in his liking for the other three activities. Never particularly successful in playing marbles against shrewd competition, it is worth noting that as a senior in high school John was one of the few boys still loyal (at least on paper) to an activity chiefly popular among ten- and eleven-year-olds.

But he was not equally immature in other fields; as we have already seen, his intellectual orientation was in some respects exceptionally mature. In a record of one week's reading, taken each semester during senior high school, John was among a minority who reported reading about foreign affairs and about political problems; he was also in a minority who did *not* read about sports. His interests in various cultural activities were persistently and genuinely on the more mature side. In an interest maturity score based on the Strong Vocational Interest Blank, John's average score in three tests given in senior high school was approximately at the eighty-fifth percentile. These inconsistencies can be more readily understood if considered in relation to John's record of late development in the physical characteristics of adolescence. In activities involving physical ability or social participation his interests were more childish than the average; in activities involving an appreciation of intellectual and cultural values he was more mature than the average.

Such irregularities in interest patterns are not difficult to comprehend when we take into account all that we know about John's development. But to his classmates, his teachers, and also to himself he sometimes presented a confusingly complex picture. John's problems of social adjustment were not made easier by the fact that at one and the same time he was too childish and too adult for most of his associates.

As he entered the senior year in high school, John's interests are well represented by his answers on a test entitled "Things You Talk About." The instructions were: "What are the things you talk about with your friends? Check each topic in the proper column, according to how often you talk about it."

TABLE 10

PERCENTAGES OF BOYS AND GIRLS DISCUSSING SPECIFIC TOPICS. THINGS THAT JOHN TALKED ABOUT "OFTEN OR VERY OFTEN"

	Books I Have Read		Art: Painting, etc.		Government, Politics, etc.		Teachers		What Happened in a Moving Picture		Movie Stars	
	B	G	B	G	B	G	B	G	B	G	B	G
Seldom or never	36	18	73	51	30	53	24	19	11	7	40	20
Sometimes	43	33	17	31	34	30	44	44	45	53	42	43
Often or very often	21	49	10	18	36	17	32	37	44	40	18	37

The columns were headed "Never," "Seldom," "Sometimes," "Often," "Very Often," and were accompanied by a list of topics covering a wide range of interests. In this test, requiring only a few minutes to take, John has given us information about himself which is closely in agreement with our records of his actual conversations with others. Table 10, listing topics that John reported talking about "often" or "very often," provides representation for his intellectual and cultural interests. Among the boys of his class, only a small minority reported, as John did, that they frequently talked about books or about art. John was also beginning to show, at this time, an interest in current events and national affairs.

While a test of this nature may truly reflect a person's leading preoccupations, it may fail to define the basic nature of an interest or the way in which it is expressed. Thus, we note that John's interest in motion pictures corresponded in degree with that of some of his acquaintances who obtained a great deal of vicarious enjoyment from the movies, but at a somewhat different intellectual level. From other records, we know that when John talked with his friends about motion pictures, it was less in terms of chatty comment on persons and episodes, and more with reference to a relatively mature interest in the motion picture as an art form, the photography, and the social ideas that might be conveyed.

TABLE 11

THINGS THAT JOHN TALKED ABOUT "SELDOM OR NEVER"

	Ball Games Outdoor Sports		Jokes		Inventions, Aeroplanes, etc.		Machines, Engines, etc.		Parties		Having Dates	
	B	G	B	G	B	G	B	G	B	G	B	G
Seldom or never	5	22	9	16	35	73	32	88	23	9	26	12
Sometimes	24	35	27	32	38	25	38	7	44	30	33	27
Often or very often	71	43	64	52	27	2	30	5	33	61	41	61

Table 11 presents topics that John talked about "Seldom" or "Never." Here we find him among the small minority of boys who rarely discussed athletics, or rarely spent time on "jokes." We also find confirmation for earlier evidence concerning his lack of mechanical interests, in which (as on many other items) he agrees more with girls than with boys.

His failure to talk about dates and parties may be on a somewhat different basis, for whatever his interest may have been we know that even as a senior in high school, he had little experience or opportunity in this area.

D. JOHN'S RELIGIOUS BELIEFS

Although we have noted a considerable degree of constancy in the several areas of interests represented in Figure 15, dramatic changes were displayed in certain other aspects of interest and attitude. As a symptom of adolescence, religious "conversion" is probably less common now than in the generation of which G. Stanley Hall wrote.[5] Sometimes, indeed, we note the opposite of conversion, in an adolescent revolt which leads to an active repudiation of religious concepts and practices. From what we have learned concerning John's other characteristics, it would not be surprising to find him following this second course toward increasing skepticism and denial.

In the eighth grade John went to the Baptist Church ("sometimes"), and to Sunday school ("regularly"). An attitude test given at this time contained questions of a multiple-choice type, permitting one or more than one answer. Without implying a comparative evaluation of the two points of view, answers on various questions were tabulated into categories indicating a "liberal" or less liberal religious attitude. In junior high school the majority of John's responses reflected beliefs that would not be classified as liberal. For example, John said he prayed: "To confess sins," "to make us safe when we die," "to cause God to change his plans," "to get God to punish our enemies." He also checked, "to think over my problems," which may be

---

[5] G. S. Hall, *Adolescence* (New York, D. Appleton and Company, 1905), Vol. II, pp. 281-362.

regarded as representing a more modern or liberal religious point of view. His other statements as to the function of prayer ("to ask Jesus for help," "to thank God for what he has done for me,") are perhaps less easy to classify, but suggest a tendency to need and to rely upon help from a source outside his immediate experiences.

Hell was to him (in junior high school) "a fiery place below the earth where the Devil rules" "a place where people pay for all the bad they've done on earth"; "a place of never ending torture." At the same time he included among his concepts of hell: "a feeling of great misery within oneself," an interpretation which may be more in line with contemporary liberal opinion.[6]

In junior high school John's concept of God was of a severe and powerful Jehovah. Success in life, he felt, was due in large part to divine intervention, "God's help" being of greater importance than "one's own handwork." In the next two years John's views on these matters changed more markedly than did those of the majority of his classmates; from a position less liberal than the average, he seemed by the tenth grade to be shifting toward an opposite extreme of opinion.

In his senior year in high school we find John asserting that "Children should be encouraged to decide their own attitudes about religion," and denying the proposition "Man cannot exist without religion." Significant is the change

---

[6] One of the most striking changes in the group as a whole was in the item, "I think of Hell as a fiery place below the earth where the Devil rules." In the eighth grade 26 per cent of the boys and 20 per cent of the girls indicated this belief. In the tenth grade only 5 per cent of each group marked the item in the same way. The tendency to select more liberal answers to religious questions in senior than in junior high school could hardly have been due to changed teaching, within this period, in the churches and Sunday schools which the boys and girls attended. In part it was probably an adolescent reaction against authority, as represented in the authoritarianism of conservative religious beliefs and practices.

which he showed in marking preference or dislike for "religious" or "irreligious people." In the tenth and eleventh grades he reported liking the former and disliking the latter, in the twelfth grade he appeared to have about equal tolerance for both, but in a test given after graduation his attitudes had completed a right about face. He now liked the "irreligious," disliked the "religious."

E. SOCIAL ATTITUDES

This does not, however, imply a "loose" attitude toward conduct and social customs. More often than most of his group, he expressed disapproval of "drinking beer," "cigarettes," "men smoking," "smoking a pipe." He was even more censorious of women smoking, but in this a large proportion of the group agreed with him. Forty-seven per cent of the boys and almost as many of the girls expressed the view that "It is worse for women to smoke cigarettes than for men." John also disliked the idea of "make-up" for girls. "Permanent waves," "using lipstick," "using rouge," seemed to him reprehensible; later, in the twelfth grade, he conceded a grudging sanction to these practices, but still indicated that he did not like them. On the lipstick issue, 11 per cent of the boys and 1 per cent of the girls agreed with him.

Among the items on the Opinion Ballot were a number which referred to aggressive [7] or rebellious behavior. John frequently expressed his endorsement of such behavior. For example, he was more willing than the majority to approve the idea of "disagreeing with my parents." More often than the group he also favored talking about himself, giving advice to people, reforming people, laughing at others, argu-

---

[7] A correlation of .48 (raised to .65 by correction for attenuation) was obtained between scores on a selection of these items and the ratings of boys on "Drive for Aggression."

ing, "doing what I want to do when I want to do it," "letting people know I don't like them."

Other sections of this case report have not indicated that John is as outspoken or overtly aggressive as this summary of his attitudes and opinions would indicate. Perhaps we can conclude, however, that he favored this course of action even though he did not always exemplify it. Although intolerant, even puritanical with regard to personal habits deviating from somewhat rigid standards, John became exceptionally liberal in attitude on various social and economic matters. His responses on the attitudes test showed a trend toward greater tolerance of other races and of minority groups. It is not surprising that he began to take the liberal side of issues involving academic freedom, free speech, and the rights and welfare of the underprivileged. At the same time, he gave evidence of being more thoughtful and more realistic about the problems that would confront him when he graduated; he was more open-minded, more flexible, less inclined to respond in the hard and fast terms of a conventional, middle-class family philosophy. If our insight were adequate to the task, we might inquire into the dynamics of the process through which a boy who entered high school with markedly conservative attitudes, graduated as a convinced and consistent liberal. Undoubtedly his high school courses had something to do with the matter. We know that he was quite definitely influenced by the social philosophy of specific teachers with whom he came in contact. But other youngsters in the same school situation reacted quite differently.

Whatever its origin, John's trend toward liberalism carried him not only beyond the opinions of his family and classmates, but also beyond the majority of his teachers. Taken as a significant aspect of social maturing, John's interests and attitudes were less an echo of his school environment than a selective response to this environment, and an expression of his own uniquely personal characteristics.

In these interests and attitudes we find evidence not only of a reasoned evolution, but also of elements of self-assertion and rebellion, consistent with the material to be presented in the next chapter, on "underlying tendencies."

Chapter VIII

AN INTERPRETATIVE STUDY OF SOME "UNDERLYING TENDENCIES"

That behavior is not always a mirror of inclination is implied in our common practice of distinguishing intentions from actions, purposes from accomplished behavior. Chapter IV of this case study gave an account of John's behavior in its more purely external aspects. Is there anything that we can learn about John's private life of wishes, motives, drives, or reaction tendencies, which will supplement what we already know about his outer behavior, and which perhaps will help to explain some of the strange inconsistencies of that behavior?

When we enter the realm of emotion and motivation, it is apparent that any single piece of evidence is more or less equivocal—pointing most plausibly, perhaps, to some particular conclusion, but conceivably also to various other interpretations. Our chief resource, in such a case, lies in the multiplication of evidence. When, as in the present instance, substantial agreement is reached by different approaches, a modest assurance may be ventured with regard to the validity of the general picture.

A. ANALYSIS OF DRIVE PATTERNS

The first approach to be presented involves the study of John's "drives" or underlying motivational tendencies, through the use of systematic ratings. These ratings were made by three staff members who could draw upon an intimate acquaintance with John over a period of from four to seven years. The ratings were designed primarily to describe significant features of his "motivational pattern," as seen by these observers, in the latter part of his adolescent period. They differ from ratings of overt behavior in that they represent a carefully considered attempt to look beneath the surface, and to utilize all available indications as to his inner characteristics. Such interpretations, frequently based upon judgments concerning subtle behavior cues, naturally involve a greater subjective factor than ratings, of, for example, "popularity." It is far easier to know a boy's actual social status, than to know how he reacts to this status, and how it accords with his often carefully concealed wishes and aspirations.[1] Following (Table 12) are the descriptions of nine "drives." The numbers after each description are ratings for John, transformed into standard scores. They are based on a consensus of judgment by three judges, and referred to the distribution of such ratings for the total sample of boys in the Adolescent Growth Study.

TABLE 12 *

DESCRIPTIONS OF "DRIVES"

Drive for Autonomy

Striving for independence and freedom; desire to be free from social ties, to shake off influence, coercion and restraint; no care for conventions and group ideology; tendency to act as one pleases.   (67)

---

[1] Nevertheless, with qualified raters, these assessments of drives have proved to be sufficiently reliable to justify their use in conjunction with other personality data. It is of course not assumed that a given "drive" represents a single fund of energy or involves any single mode of expression of a unitary trait. A drive rating is, rather, an observer's subjectively averaged impression of the strength of an individual's urges, purposes, or motives as classified under a specified psychological category. For the development and analysis of this technique, see E. Frenkel-Brunswik, "Motivation and Behavior," *Genetic Psychology Monographs*, Vol. 26, 1942, pp. 121-265.

* These formulations were adapted from the discussion of "needs" in H. A. Murray, *Explorations in Personality* (New York, Oxford University Press, 1938), xiv + 761 pp.

TABLE 12 (*Continued*)

Drive for Social Ties, Social Acceptance

Desire to be generally well-liked; to conform to custom, to join groups, to live sociably, to be accepted by a group in any form, to make contacts. (57)

Drive for Achievement

Desire to attain a high standard of objective accomplishments; to increase self-regard by successful exercise of talent, to select hard tasks; ambitious; high aspiration level. (Rating scale starts from "no desire to accomplish something outstanding," and ends with "excessive demands on himself.") (58)

Drive for Recognition

Desire to excite praise and commendation, to command respect; social approval and prestige, honors and fame. (64)

Drive for Abasement

Tendency to self-depreciation, self-blame or belittlement; to submit passively to external forces, to accept injury, blame, criticism, punishment; tendency to become resigned to fate, to admit inferiority and defeat, to confess, to seek punishment and misfortune; masochism. (59)

Drive for Aggression

Desire to attack others; by belittling, depriving, ridiculing, depreciating. (57)

Drive for "Succorance"

Desire for support from outside; from people, institutions, or supernatural agencies. (57)

Drive for Control (Dominance)

Desire to control one's human environment, by suggestion, persuasion or command. (59)

Drive for Escape

Tendency to escape all unpleasant situations; to avoid blame, hardship, etc., to project own failures on others or on circumstances; to be unable to sacrifice immediate pleasure to future ends; to indulge in fantasy, etc. (47)

As we look at these measures, we are struck by the fact that John is credited with having strong drives; his scores are above the group average of 50 in eight of the nine drive traits. But we also note that these tendencies to action are in very poor agreement with our impressions of his actual overt behavior. John's extreme high score for "autonomy" is in contrast with the faltering unassertiveness often recorded in our narrative comments and ratings.[2] His drive for social ties is equally in contrast with surface indications of quite unsociable habits. We have seen also that John has frequently vexed others by a pestering inaptitude which would seem to fit poorly with a marked desire for achievement and recognition. Thus it would appear that John's conduct has been unable to fulfill his own demands; it is not surprising that he was rated as "unhappy," and "maladjusted," when this discrepancy existed between what he wanted to do and what he was actually able to accomplish.

But there is also a noticeable discrepancy among the drives themselves. It is not usual to find a strong demand for "autonomy" together with a need for social ties. The latter drive may be considered an explanation of John's frequent presence at social gatherings in which, however, he was more commonly a fringing observer than an actual participant. The desire for social ties was likewise the source of his persistent though inconspicuous attempts to find acceptance, and his patient though unsuccessful endeavor to master the accepted social techniques. It was John's misfortune that this urge was so frequently in conflict with a recurrent demand for independence. He could not be as egocentric as he was, and at the same time find any direct and adequate expression of his striving for social contacts and affiliations.

A second marked conflict in John's drives appears in the

---

[2] See Chapter IV, *supra.*

drives for "succorance" and for "aggression." The former is shown in John's emotional dependence on family and friends. Superimposed upon this dependence are his aggressive tendencies. The interference of the two may account for the fact that John's aggression does not usually reveal itself directly in his behavior, but finds expression predominantly in satirical humor. Occasionally his aggression breaks forth in open hostility, but on the whole, our behavioral records show him to be submissive. These facts are especially interesting in the face of the agreement of the three judges on his underlying aggressiveness, and in view of the more common tendency (in the group as a whole) for aggression to be associated with active dominant behavior. The counteraction of aggression by strongly opposed tendencies may, in a general way, account for the "inhibited" character of the picture presented by the behavior history. On ratings involving overt expressiveness, emotional buoyancy, freedom from inhibition, and freedom from tenseness, John's scores over a six-year period were for the most part below the twentieth percentile; and frequently below the fifth percentile (Chapter IV). This conflict is somewhat more frequent, in the group as a whole, than the conflict between Autonomy and Social Ties. But though aggression and succorance may occur together they can rarely avoid conflicting with each other. To seek support and direction, and at the same time to have an underlying hostility, must result in inconsistent (ambivalent) attitudes toward people.

Furthermore, the ratings of John indicate a juxtaposition of a rather strong drive for "abasement" and a great need for recognition. John's tendency toward self-abasement is revealed most clearly in the persistent occurrence of acts in which he provokes maltreatment, resulting (one may suppose) in a more complete feeling of inadequacy. In a rational world, being humiliated is not ordinarily regarded as a forward step in the direction of being favorably recognized. It is of course possible that his willingness to accept humiliation was in part a defense against a *defeated drive* for prestige, but there are many points in which these drives are so incompatible that we can expect to find no simple explanation of their existence together in the same individual.

In John's conflicting pattern of drives, the most positive feature seems to be his drive for achievement, which is apparently capable of motivating concentrated and serious work. The combination of this strong drive with a relatively weak tendency toward "escape" is unusual in the group as a whole, and may indicate exceptional staying-power in dealing with difficult tasks. It would also indicate, however, that John's interest should be encouraged in fields in which his actual or potential abilities are compatible with his desire to achieve. Such encouragement is wiser than a too zealous attempt to promote social activities; in John's case, the more hopeful avenue to social adjustment would seem to lie through gaining self-confidence as a result of recognized achievement. John's freedom from escape tendencies has not been equally marked at all times; particularly in the tenth grade, at around the age of sixteen, he showed many symptoms of withdrawal and of temporarily "giving up." His ability to recover from this phase, to meet issues and to keep trying, may be a favorable sign for the future.

Upon the origin of John's motivational patterns some light is thrown by data concerning his family, although our information in this respect is less complete than could be desired. Our knowledge of the attitude of his parents, especially of his mother, is of some use in this connection. It is apparent that John was kept overlong in infantile dependence, even in somewhat humiliating circumstances with respect to his mother's detailed control over his activities. It is possible to understand, from this, his striving for a continued status of dependence and support, as well as his reaction against it, with related tendencies of aggression and hostility. Perhaps we can also understand his tendency toward abasement (induced by a dominating mother) coupled with a compensatory striving for position and prestige. These conflicting tendencies, together with John's specific abilities and disabilities may be among the factors contributing to his originality in thinking and in various aspects of creative expression. A critical problem is whether in the future these conflicts will continue to stimulate effort on his part, or will become so great that he will be less free for independent achievement.

The organization of John's drives as construed by those who know him suggests that the picture of a listless and indifferent boy, given repeatedly in observational ratings, refers only to a surface phenomenon; and that there are beneath the surface strongly active inner strivings blocked from revealing themselves in any adequate way. John's tenseness provides an intimation of this, but it can only be understood in terms of his total motivational pattern.

As shown in the case of John, a statement about a certain motivation (for example, John's drive for recognition or for aggression) does not in itself imply a directly corresponding behavioral technique. Thus we may distinguish conceptually two aspects of the personality, the one representing the displayed techniques, the other representing underlying factors in behavior. Fantasy reactions and self-reports will often be determined to a greater extent by the latter than by the former. For a full comprehension of the personality, both are important. Since we cannot consider displayed behavior a direct copy of the underlying motives in a one-to-one relationship, we have to look for more complex ways in which drives receive expression in overt conduct. This is one of the essential problems of the nature or the structure of personality, and cannot be neglected in any comprehensive study of the individual.

B. ANALYSIS OF PROJECTIVE MATERIALS; STORIES

Another approach to the study of John's "private world of meanings, significances, patterns and feelings"[3] is through the use of various types of records of creative activity. Such records, there is good reason to believe, often give revealing indications of characteristics not always directly or openly expressed.

In John's junior year in high school, he took a "Thema Test," in which a series of pictures were shown to him[4] and he supplied a story to explain each picture. Using these materials only, tentative interpretations were made by two members of the Institute staff who had no personal acquaintance with John. It would be instructive to present John's actual stories, together with the detailed interpretations and the organizing principles employed in reaching these interpretations. Since this is not possible in the present case report, we shall confine ourselves to a brief summary, which the reader can compare with information about John derived from other sources, more especially with the drive ratings reported above.

Interpretation[5] of Responses to the Murray Pictures

This boy has some artistic sensibility and creativity, but his associations to the Murray pictures are so unusual that he tends to make things seem absurd; he is at home in the realm of the bizarre and

---

[3] L. K. Frank, "Projective Methods for the Study of Personality," *Journal of Psychology*, Vol. 8, 1939, pp. 389-413.

[4] The Murray Thematic Apperception Test, in a form modified by H. E. Jones. Fifteen of the Morgan-Murray pictures were used, with three additional pictures; the subjects were shown the pictures on a screen in a darkened room.

[5] By R. N. Sanford.

fantastic. It may be inferred that he has strong hostile impulses, associated in part with rebellious, revolutionary ideas. This rebellion can be interpreted as a defiance of conscience, an attempt to overcome his superego with its deeply ingrained family sanctions. Opposed to this rejection of his family, with the accompanying patterns of jesting or teasing cynicism and with well-defined sadistic impulses, we note indications that he is afraid of his own emotions, and that there remains a deference toward his family with dependent, submissive tendencies approaching masochism. His present pessimistic attitudes are those of "a mother's boy gone sour." The outlook for a better adjustment rests upon his success, in college or in adult life, in achieving a more genuine independence from his family, and in finding a sphere of occupation within which his excellent abilities can be realistically employed.

In a part of this test, repeated a year later, John furnished an elaborate story in response to one of the Murray pictures. An interpretation [6] follows:

It is probable that no one can read this story and not have the impression that intense emotion pervades it. Not only is the emotion intense, but it follows a pattern different from that shown by any other member of the group. Annoyance, irritation, rebellion, sadness, self-pity, meditation, often occur in the story, together with a uniquely violent degree of aggression and hostility. Under the guise of telling a story, John apparently "lets go"; he is going to tell a "wild one" without any sense to it, and put on a good show.... He apparently does not realize that the remote impersonality of his verbal expression, coupled with the bizarre nature of the story's content, conveys immediately to the reader that which he would conceal.... The story is about a boy whose family is totally unable to control him. He goes berserk and the family is described as powerless to do anything about it. This is most strange, for usually adults can control children in some way, if only by superior force. We may think of this, in a measure, as representing John's own wishful thinking. *In fantasy, he expresses through the boy's action how he himself would like to behave toward his own family.* He expresses hostile feelings that ordinarily are not shown, since their very nature would bring him punishment and loss of support. In fantasy, the boy is powerfully dominant, the family submissive and indulgent. We may tentatively infer that in actuality John's family is dominant, and he is submissive. The attitudes expressed here are probably not transitory, not merely incidental to the test situation. They represent, rather, a deep-seated part of John's habitual

[6] By Wilma Lloyd.

response. They are attitudes that partially determine how he looks upon the world. It seems more than likely that in his choice of fantasy materials, he has revealed a primary source of his conflict, his relationships with his family.

As a consequence of these relationships, we may feel that John has developed too great demands on himself and his world; these are out of all proportion to his chances for satisfaction. He has excellent intelligence, though it may not be functioning to capacity. He is sensitive, aware of objects in their relationships in a highly differentiated way, yet unable to respond adequately in terms of what he knows. His strengths are in terms of his capacity for logical procedures and for analysis. But he sees too many sides of a question to act promptly, and is apt to be indecisive. We may infer that he is slow in adapting to changing situations, somewhat rigid and inflexible. In these respects he conforms to the conventional picture of the "introvert"; his aspirations, however, are incompatible with other factors in his personality and in his immediate social environment. Unable to realize these aspirations, he becomes resentful, antagonistic and hostile towards both himself and his world.[7]

To the interpretations based on the foregoing sources, we may add two other discussions of John's underlying tendencies, based respectively upon a voice record and upon two Rorschach (ink-blot) tests. The technique for obtaining and analyzing the voice record has been described elsewhere.[8]

C. ANALYSIS OF VOICE RECORDS [9]

This young man has a low voice with considerable chest register, but with a tendency to "break" or switch into an almost pure head

---

[7] "John reveals in this story a high degree of emotional conflict. The emotional pattern seems clear, as well as certain of the dynamisms developed in an attempt to resolve the conflict. Depersonalization seems deeply imbedded; he uses projection to a great extent; rationalization and 'objectivity' characterize his intellectual approach; he fulfills in fantasy his wishes for power and self-aggrandizement; he uses the comic in depreciation of others. It is unlikely that John shows in other forms of behavior as open an expression of the forces that direct him. He is too inhibited."

[8] H. E. Jones, and P. J. Moses, "The Analysis of Voice Records," *Journal of Consulting Psychology*, Vol. 6, 1942, pp. 255-261.

[9] The analysis was made by Dr. Paul Moses, who interpreted the record "blind," that is, with no other information describing the subject. Age: eighteen.

register. His articulation is slipshod, except when he is self-consciously performing. An element of fearfulness or anxiety is exhibited by the absence of relation between pitch at the beginning and at the end of sentences. Effeminacy is indicated by a "glissando," avoiding concentration on one single pitch. Self-consciousness is shown by the exaggerated duration of vowels. It may be noted also that while some accents are emphasized, there is no genuine support for such emphasis; it is superficial and not confirmed by underlying factors. There is no vocal expression of whole-hearted enthusiasm. His pathos tries to move others to sympathy, not unsuccessfully; the playing with registers is too obvious. . . . Evidences of withdrawal are shown by the tendency of the speech melody to lower into the "lowest depths." These are like hiding places, and the whole procedure reminds one of withdrawal. There is also a sadistic component suggested by the raising and sudden lowering of the melody. A certain rigidity is present. He thinks about himself and makes himself the center of the world. He is boundlessly sensitive. He is, however, not solitary, for he needs people around, if only to show them up and tease or torment them. From his voice we may infer an asthenic body structure, with a relatively small chest diameter. Turning to the content of his speech, the "danse macabre" of his fantastic ideas reveals immature attitudes (a tendency toward infantile destructiveness). He is, however, intelligent and gifted. I would infer that he is not precise in his work. He is ambitious, in an unsocial way. This is by far the most interesting record of the whole group, but in some respects depressing to contemplate.

D. ANALYSIS OF RORSCHACH RECORDS

John was a subject for a Rorschach Test in his fifteenth year (ninth grade) and again three years later. These tests have been interpreted [10] as follows:

The Rorschach record obtained when John was eighteen is not one of a well-adjusted young man. On the contrary, one may infer that his emotional life is quite disturbed, strong, labile, and self-centered. The intelligence seems to be superior and is indirectly affected by the emotional tension. It may be expected that this will result in a somewhat uneven intellectual level, with performances which are sometimes very superior but are frequently unsystematic. The boy is probably irritable

---

[10] The records were analyzed "blind" by Dr. Zygmunt Piotrowski. As in the case in Dr. Moses' analysis, he had never seen John and had no information beyond that contained in the specific test record.

and has great difficulty in making an effortless and satisfactory emotional adjustment to his environment. His superior intelligence and his strong inner life (inner creativeness) serve to stabilize his labile affectivity. He seeks to get along with his environment but he does so less by trying consciously to control himself than by cautious cleverness and calculated behavior (including affectation).

The chief psychological problem as seen in the Rorschach seems to be the great tension caused by the existence of opposite tendencies. On the one hand, there seems to be a great capacity for the enjoyment of strong emotions and for letting himself go emotionally, but on the other hand we note definite evidence of a tendency to avoid situations which could arouse strong emotions, and a tendency to inhibit certain emotions. Strong tensions may be expected to result from these opposite tendencies. This inner conflict also seems to affect the boy's fundamental attitude toward the world and toward his own future; he is apparently hesitating between assuming an active and outgoing attitude and assuming an attitude of submission and resignation. He has, however, enough control and enough inner life to be able, in large measure, to hide the conflict from others. This young man's creative imagination and his productive inner life seem to be better organized and developed than his direct emotional relations to the environment. When one considers only his intellectual and educational achievement, he makes a much better impression than when his direct emotional relations with people are considered.

The conflict from which he seems to be suffering is probably a very old one. One receives the impression that he has changed in the last five years. At fifteen he seems to have been more rigid, more precise, and more repressed than he is at eighteen. Of importance would seem to be the great increase in affective life and the increased interest in relations with his fellow human beings, a change which certainly is desirable. I believe that this is a young man who deserves help and who, if he continues to improve, will probably be a useful and creative person.

It is instructive to compare the several interpretations given above in Sections B, C and D. Imperfect agreement would be expected, in view of the imperfect reliability and validity of interpretations based on single examples or single modes of creative expression. Somewhat different emphases would be expected. But the consistency of these analyses with each other, and with information derived from other sources, is at least suggestive as to the possible uses of such records in the study of the individual case. No inferences, however, as to the general validity of projective methods can be drawn from data of this nature. A subject such as John Sanders, with strongly marked and somewhat deviate characteristics, may be expected to provide more significant material for projective analyses than could be found in the general run of cases. It is probably also true that the different projective methods will be of unequal value for different individuals, and that the course of wisdom is to use more than one method, in combination with other data from the life history, rather than to rely upon interpretations based on a single approach.

E. EMOTIONAL TRENDS AS REVEALED BY A PHYSIOLOGICAL TECHNIQUE [11]

An instrumental approach to the study of emotional organization is furnished by a familiar laboratory procedure which involves the photographic recording of the "galvanic skin reaction." It is well known that in terms of averages for groups of subjects, the magnitude of this reaction varies widely according to the emotional potency of the stimuli.[12] It is also known that when we turn from the comparison of

---

[11] For this purpose a galvanometer, Wheatstone Bridge, and photo-recorder were used. The laboratory arrangements in the present study are described in the following two reports: H. E. Jones, "An Experimental Cabinet for Physiological Studies of Emotions," *Child Development,* Vol. 7, 1936, pp. 183-188; N. W. Shock, "A Continuous Recorder for Obtaining Synchronous Curves of Physiological Responses to Stimuli in Human Subjects," *Child Development, loc. cit.,* pp. 169-182.

[12] One method of expressing reactions is in terms of the amount of change, in ohms, in the apparent resistance of the skin following the presentation of a stimulus. Emotionally significant terms, whether pleasant or unpleasant, are *on the average* readily distinguished from neutral or indifferent terms. This is illustrated in the following results from an association test given to forty eleventh-grade boys. The first three items were classified by the boys as "indifferent," the second three as either strongly pleasant or strongly un-

stimuli, for the group as a whole, to the study of individual differences among the members of the group, a wide range occurs from "reactive" to relatively "non-reactive" individuals. Some persons tend to respond only in a small degree even to stimuli which are highly provocative for the general run of cases.

Our first tendency is to infer that these low-reactive persons are exceptionally unemotional, placid, or stable, since in terms of this particular criterion of autonomic response, they are relatively free from indications of inner disturbance. Such a conclusion, however, overlooks the fact that individual patterns exist in which a restriction of this aspect of internal response is often accompanied by exaggerated symptoms of maladjustment in other areas.[13]

Within the present study, a comparison was made [14] between twenty boys and girls who presented consistently low reactions on the galvanometer and twenty who at the other extreme presented consistently high reactions, in experimental situations extending over a six-year period. The stimulus factors included association words, questions from emotional inventories, and various other types of ideational and physical stimuli. In terms of wholly independent criteria, based on observational ratings in social situations (cf.

---

pleasant. In presenting the items, they were given in a rotating order so as to avoid effects due to position in series:

Stimulus Term	Average Reaction in Ohms
Waste basket	230
Shirt Sleeve	436
Table cloth	557
Castor oil	936
Bad habit	964
Sweetheart	1130

[13] H. E. Jones, "The Galvanic Skin Reflex as Related to Overt Emotional Expression," *American Journal of Psychology*, Vol. 47, 1935, pp. 241-251.

[14] H. E. Bramble, *A Study of Apparent Changes in Skin Resistance as Related to Certain Behavior Traits in Adolescents*, M. A. Thesis, University of California, 1942.

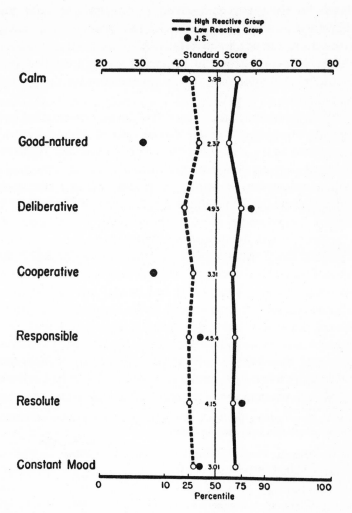

Fig. 17.—Analysis of Mean Differences Between Extreme Groups

Chapter IV) the low-reactive cases showed emotional patterns which were on the whole less mature than those commonly characteristic of the high reactive cases. This is illustrated in Figure 17, which shows (in standard scores) that the low-reactive cases were judged to be less calm, less good-natured, impulsive rather than deliberative, uncoöperative, irresponsible, indecisive and inconstant as to mood. This formidable array of unfavorable characteristics may be compared with the generally favorable profile presented by the "high-reactive" cases. The numbers between the two profiles (3.98, 2.37, etc.) are critical ratios for the difference, in a specified trait, between the averages of the two contrasting groups. These critical ratios indicate a reliable difference in every trait except "good-naturedness," and even here the chances are 99 out of 100 of a true difference in the direction indicated.

It would appear that a tendency toward moderate or marked reactions (in this particular response area) is a sign of a better balanced emotional organization than a tendency toward low or completely inhibited reactions, which so often are accompanied by overt behavior earning the description of "excitable," "irritable," "emotionally disturbed," etc.

Some interest, then, attaches to the record made by John in repeated experimental sessions. He was not one of those classified as consistently non-reactive, nor would we expect him to be such in view of our frequent notations of external behavior which was judged to be relatively inhibited and unexpressive. But he sometimes showed a tendency toward restricted reaction as recorded by the galvanometer; this became particularly marked in the ninth and tenth grades, when John's records placed him among our least reactive cases.[15] In preceding chapters we have noted that this part of

---

[15] To 30 items of a personal-social inventory, given in the low ninth grade, John gave only four responses as high as the group average. Similar

John's school career was marked by an exceptional accumulation of physical handicaps, social defeats, and emotional idiosyncrasies. Did he, at this time, resemble the "low-reactive" group in personality traits? For the traits included in Figure 17, the larger black circles represent the ratings of John Sanders, transformed into standard scores. These measures are based on observations during the middle part of the ninth and tenth grade period. As in the case of ratings of other members of the group, they were made independently by three or more judges who had no knowledge of the physiological data or of the classifications based on these data. In five of the seven traits shown in this chart, John's score was either close to or lower than the average of the twenty "low-reactive" cases. In two characteristics, however, he failed to conform; his tendency to be deliberate rather than impulsive, and his basic "resoluteness," remained in evidence even at this time when other traits had become organized into a decidedly different pattern.

Previous chapters have indicated that when John reached his senior year in high school he was well on his way toward solving many of his major problems. With the record of generally better adjustment in the twelfth grade, it is interesting to note that his instrumental records also show a change. No longer a "low-reactor," he was now similar, in the instrumental record, to the "high-reactive" group.[16] At the same time the ratings of John's overt behavior moved

results were obtained in the following year. Both on inventory items and on association words, he tended to give "zero reactions" (absence of any measurable change in the instrumental record) approximately twice as often as was true of the group as a whole. His average response on association words was less than one-third of the group average.

[16] In the association words John's average response was three times as high as the group mean, and he now gave only 25 per cent zero responses, as compared with a group mean of 33 per cent. In the personal-social inventory, while many zero responses still occurred, John's average reaction was more than three times as high as his average recorded three years earlier.

out of the unfavorable zone in such traits as good-natured-ness, coöperativeness, and responsibility. This evidence of a better balanced emotional pattern concurs with our other available information concerning changes in John's personal characteristics during the latter part of adolescence.

Chapter IX

JOHN AS HE SAW HIMSELF

A. RESULTS FROM A PERSONAL-SOCIAL INVENTORY

John's attitudes toward himself, his more or less articulate appraisals of his own status, may be gleaned from various interviews and written reports. The source which offers the most clearly comparable evidence, for successive years, consists of his responses to a Personal-Social Inventory.[1] It is of course recognized that any attempt to interpret a person's self-report, on schedules of this type, should rest in part upon our knowledge of the faithfulness with which the report was made. A different value must be given to responses which are carefully and thoughtfully produced, than to answers which are hasty, ill-considered, or which involve an incompletely coöperative attitude. In the case of John Sanders, our records[2] show that he took this personal inventory seriously, and attempted to give discriminating answers. In analyzing results, especial attention has been directed to unusual or deviate responses. These were classified as follows: (a) responses which were atypical as com-

---

[1] Administered yearly for seven years, beginning in the high fifth or low sixth grade. Together with several additional series of items, the Inventory included a number of sections from tests reported by Rogers, and by Symonds and Jackson. See C. R. Rogers, *Measuring Personality Adjustment in Children Nine to Thirteen Years of Age*, Teachers College Contributions to Education, No. 458 (1931), v + 107 pp.; P. M. Symonds and C. E. Jackson, "An Adjustment Survey," *Journal of Educational Research*, Vol. 21, 1930, pp. 321-330.

[2] The evidence is based on records made by observers during the testing situation, and also on the consistency of his responses in successive years.

pared with the records of John's classmates; (*b*) responses which were in disagreement with the picture of John as given by his classmates or by adult acquaintances; and (*c*) responses which seemed superficially inconsistent with other statements made by himself on the same schedule.

Among the tendencies which became apparent in this material are the following:

1. The acknowledgment, to a very unusual degree, of personal deficiencies.
2. The expression, on the other hand, of somewhat extravagant wishes to be outstanding in a wide range of personal characteristics.
3. The use of various protective devices, singly or in combination: fantasy, self-inflation, denial of emotional involvement, and, at critical times, the denial of deficiencies which at other times were freely admitted.

1. DEFICIENCIES

A number of items in the Inventory are in the following form:

Read the sentences below, and the questions that follow them. If the answer to a question is "yes," put a check mark on "yes." If the answer is "no," put a mark on "no." If the true answer is somewhere between yes and no, put the mark where it will be most true.

B. is a big strong boy who can beat any of the other boys in a fight.

Am I just like him? | YES | | | | | | | | | NO |

In scoring responses, the cells from left to right were numbered 1 to 10. A score of 1 would indicate strong similarity and a score of 10 strong dissimilarity to the example given. Examples of additional items:

D. is the best ball-player in school. . . .

G. is a leader. All of the fellows do what he tells them. . . .

J. is the most popular boy in school. . . .

K. has more girl friends than any of the other fellows. . . .

To the five items above John gave similar answers in the sixth and seventh grades, his average self-rating being near the middle of the Yes—No scale (5.2). He had no delusions about enjoying a favored status, but neither did he appear to consider that his status was particularly unfavorable. In the eighth grade, however, he began to admit deficiencies which had already been only too apparent to others. On these five items his average rating was now 8.4, or close to the negative extreme. Previous chapters have indicated that in the ninth grade John's physical immaturity was most conspicuous, and that he was having an increased struggle to obtain any kind of social recognition. The downward trend in actual status, from the eighth to the ninth grade, was countered by a slight upward trend in his self-report, to an average value of 7. In the tenth and subsequent grades, however, he veered back toward the admission of extremely unfavorable status. For the most part, it would appear that he was alert and candid in the appraisal of his own deficiencies, although he may have protected himself to some extent by drawing a more favorable picture than was actually justified, both in the seventh grade when his status was showing sudden signs of deteriorating, and in the ninth grade when it had reached an extremely low point.

On one other item John rated himself consistently, and not inaccurately, near the negative extreme:

N. has more spending money than the other boys. Am I just like him?

He did not, however, consider that he was markedly dissimilar to "R., a boy who can dance better than any boy in school," or to "S., the best dressed boy in school." On these items his average self-rating was near the middle of the scale. He also placed himself near the middle position on items involving school grades, and "brightness" in school.

Another group of items, to be answered more directly "yes or no," was concerned with sources of worry or anxiety. It was infrequent for boys to give a frankly affirmative answer to these direct questions. In the sixth grade John proved himself to be one of the exceptions by admitting that he "often felt blue," that he was "often very lonely," that he "got upset easily," that he "sometimes wished he had never been born," and that he considered himself "a rather nervous person." [3] A year later he omitted these perhaps too-revealing statements, but checked one which would indicate a similar state of mind, that is, that he was "often terribly unhappy." After the seventh grade John, like the majority of his classmates, refrained from making such direct admissions about his feelings. As late as the eleventh or twelfth grades, however, he responded affirmatively to the following questions:

> Do you worry about things you have done that you have never told anyone about?
>
> Do you worry a long time after something has happened to make you feel silly or embarrassed?
>
> Do you sometimes feel the things you do are of little importance?
>
> Do you sometimes feel very happy and then suddenly very sad without knowing why?

John's sense of his own deficiencies is clearly expressed by his score in the category "Personal Inferiority," based on the items discussed above and other similar items. In every year except one (low seventh grade) John was in the highest 5 per cent of the group with regard to admitted inferiorities; in the tenth and eleventh grades his score in this respect was at the extreme end of the distribution. The evidence in this section is in agreement with that based on independent sources.

---

[3] Percentages of boys making similar answers, in the sixth grade, on each of these five items: 18, 23, 8, 23, 11.

2. Aspirations

On each of the items listed on p. 132, an additional question was asked, viz.:

D. is the best ball-player in school. Do I wish to be just like him?

In response, one could indicate, by a rating of 1, an extremely high valuation on this type of ability, or, by a rating of 10, an extreme negative attitude toward such an accomplishment. More common were intermediate ratings indicating a more moderate aspiration in one direction or the other. John's professed aspirations were extreme. He not only wished to be "just like" the best ball-player in school, but also to be equal to the biggest and strongest, the brightest, the best dancer, the best-dressed, the most popular, and the most outstanding leader. In the tenth grade, a period when we have seen other evidences of withdrawal from competition, his aspirations became somewhat more restrained, but again in the eleventh and twelfth grades they were outstandingly high.[4] These responses were unusual not only because of the insistent demand to be at the top, but also because of the demand to excel in so many different fields of activity. More typically, John's classmates tended to select specific areas in which they wished to be outstanding, the areas differing as they matured and as their values changed. During the first three years of the study, boys very commonly wished to excel in physical prowess. At that time they indicated no desire to have many girl friends, to be surpassingly good dancers, or to be well

_____

[4] An exception was John's record with regard to wanting to be like "K., who has more girl friends than any of the other fellows." In this item, his aspiration ratings, from the sixth to the twelfth grade, were successively 1, 5, 9, 9, 6, 3 and 1. An increasing negative attitude toward the opposite sex, reaching a peak in the eighth and ninth grades, suggests a conventional though delayed "latent period."

dressed. In the next two years their interests turned rather definitely in these directions, and in addition they wished to be popular and to be leaders. By the time they reached the second year in senior high school there are indications of a general decrease in the value attached to physical prowess, popularity, leadership, and appearance; the tendency of the group was to wish to be above average but not to be outstanding in these respects. The only aspirations John shared consistently with the group were "to be bright" and "to get good marks." As a group the boys did not relinquish these scholarly or pseudo-scholarly aspirations, although for the most part they were more moderate than John in expressed desires. The lack of discrimination shown by John with respect to his aspirations would appear to indicate a wish to be outstanding *per se*, without much regard to the field in which recognition might be achieved.

Another item giving the opportunity to express ambitions was the question, "When you are grown up, what sort of a person do you want to be?" Table 13 lists four alternative answers, with the percentages of boys and of girls choosing each answer at each grade level.

The first of the above answers, representing a degree of ambition not at all compatible with John's prospects or abilities, was given by him in the sixth, seventh, and eighth grades. In the ninth and tenth grades he moderated his demands to becoming a leader in whatever town he lived in; finally, in the last two years of high school, he became resigned (perhaps more realistically) to the ambition shared by most of his classmates of being "a happy ordinary person with a good job."

From one point of view we cannot help but admire John's persistent drive to "amount to something." It is only by accident that great things can grow from lowly aspirations. But when too marked a discrepancy develops between what

TABLE 13

VOCATIONAL ASPIRATIONS: PERCENTAGES OF BOYS AND GIRLS °

Item	Group	Grade						
		6	7	8	9	10	11	12
"I want to be a very great person and do great things that people will talk about."	Boys	10	11	13	13	15	13	20
	Girls	4	7	8	10	14	11	10
"I want to be one of the leaders in whatever town I live in."	Boys	1	3	4	8	10	14	8
	Girls	1	4	0	3	1	1	4
"I want to be a happy ordinary person with a good job."	Boys	75	80	79	77	72	72	72
	Girls	87	85	89	83	81	89	85
"I would rather not grow up."	Boys	14	6	4	3	3	3	1
	Girls	7	4	3	1	0	1	1

* Based on 71 boys and 72 girls who took the test for seven consecutive years.

a person is and what he wants to be, the contrast may retard rather than stimulate effort. In John's case, this apparent discrepancy became very large in the eighth grade.[5] In the ninth grade, a part of his adjustment to adverse circumstances consisted in denying the degree of deficiency, and thus bringing aspiration closer to actuality. In the tenth grade, a more realistic adjustment was made by admitting the deficiencies but reducing the level of aspiration. In the twelfth grade, which was marked by many external evidences of improved adjustment, the discrepancy between self and ideal was again very large; while wanting, for example, to be the most popular boy in school and the best ball player, he regarded himself (quite correctly) as one of the least popular and as one of the poorest at playing ball.

[5] A classification was made of the percentage of 41 items on which the discrepancy was large between self and ideal. In John's case this percentage, in successive years from the sixth to the twelfth grade, was 22, 11, 36, 25, 14, 44, 42. Note the decline in the ninth and tenth grades.

But such discrepancies, in the spheres of social and of athletic achievement, were less important to him now than formerly. Other means of self-expression were beginning to bring their own unique rewards. (Chapters III, IV.)

Another aspect of aspiration, containing an element of fantasy, can be found in John's responses to the following item:

Suppose that just by wishing you could change yourself into any sort of person.... Which of these people would you wish to be?

From twenty-six possible choices, three selections were to be made. The more important choices are listed in Table 14, with the percentage of boys making a given selection in a given year. A decline is apparent in the glamor-appeal of being a detective, a cowboy or an inventor, and an increase in the more prosaic choice of lawyer, business man and engineer. As would be expected from what we know concerning his mechanical interests (Chapter VII), John never made the choice of inventor or engineer. Nor, with his physical make-up, did he choose policeman or cowboy.

TABLE 14

PERCENTAGES OF BOYS CHOOSING AN ACTIVITY *

	Grade						
	6	7	8	9	10	11	12
Teacher	0	0	1	3	1	4	6
Policeman	0	4	0	0	4	7	10
King	7	1	1	1	7	1	10
Movie Star	8	10	8	11	17	14	21
Doctor	18	18	14	15	20	18	21
Detective	39	39	30	35	25	13	6
Cowboy	39	38	28	10	10	6	8
Inventor	27	23	37	21	14	21	15
Lawyer	8	14	14	11	11	15	17
Business man	20	24	25	37	39	45	41
Engineer	20	28	30	49	48	45	48

* Based on 71 cases who took the test for seven consecutive years.

But his three most persistent nominations in the above list are even more divergent from anything in his own background of potentialities; these were (1) to be a movie star, (2) to be a detective, and (3) to be a "king." John's professed interest in being a detective is perhaps hard to explain, except in terms of a delayed maturity. His choices of "movie star" and "king" are even more fantastic; they illustrate the magnitude as well as the inappropriateness of his wish-fulfilling ambitions.

In the preceding chapter, dealing with John's dominant pattern of motives and underlying tendencies, it was noted that in his relations with others he frequently exhibited a strong drive for achievement and a strong drive for recognition (p. 115). These drives were more often frustrated than fulfilled. It is not surprising that they have found expression, in frank and exaggerated form, in his inner life of fantasy.

3. Family Relationships

John's relation to his father involved a more comradely understanding than could usually be achieved with his mother. It was his father who indulged him in an occasional game of dominoes, or a story, before going to bed. It was his father who had comforted him when, on vividly remembered occasions in earlier childhood, a recurring dream terrified him and sent him scurrying to his parents' room. Mrs. Sanders seemed to regard these dreams as vaguely reprehensible, but Mr. Sanders was usually ready with practical sympathy.

In one of the sections of the Personal-Social Inventory, John was given an opportunity to express his "wishes" about a variety of matters involving general social relationships. For five years he checked the items "I wish my father had more time to spend with me," "I wish my father and mother were not so busy all the time," and "I wish my mother could be happier." He also noted, on several occasions, "I wish my mother agreed more with modern children's ideas," "I wish my father were more cheerful," "I wish my parents would have more patience with me," and "I wish I did not quarrel so much with my family." At the age of 13, one of his principal wishes was "to have my father and mother love me more"; at the age of 17, "to be grown-up and get away from home."

Other items give repeated indication of tension over the strict rules and restraints which, we know, were for the most part set up by his mother, and somewhat doubtfully approved by Mr. Sanders. From the Inventory as well as from other sources we gain an impression of John's home life as lacking in some of the supporting factors which would have helped him to gain a happy and secure confidence in his own status during the troubled period of adolescence. Perhaps this is an understatement, for quite evidently the home situation in itself was one of the primary agencies in making his adolescence a troubled one.

4. Attitudes Toward School

We have seen that although John had a great deal of difficulty with some of his school subjects, and was by no means uniformly popular with his teachers, the school was not for him a major area of maladjustment. This is shown in his responses to a test containing approximately fifty items, and entitled "Things You Do Not Like About School." [6]

The instructions were:

"Pick out the things you do not like about school. Some people dislike a lot of things about school; others may think school is just right

---

[6] These items were derived chiefly from the Symonds-Jackson adjustment survey (*op. cit.*).

as it is. Check on the dotted line those things which you do not like about school—things that you would change if you could."

John marked fewer of these items than most of his classmates. Table 15 lists a number of items which he selected fairly consistently, together with the percentage of boys and of girls who agreed with him, in any given year, in disliking the item in question.

The last item in Table 15 ("Having certain pupils run everything in school") was in general more of a source of disturbance to girls than to boys, particularly in the senior high school period when cliques were most ubiquitous in

TABLE 15

PERCENTAGES OF BOYS AND GIRLS DISLIKING ASPECTS OF SCHOOL LIFE

		Grade						
		6	7	8	9	10	11	12
"Teachers who have the wrong opinion about you."	Boys	30	55	55	52	58	58	51
	Girls	28	47	57	51	43	54	36
"Being punished for things one does not do."	Boys	69	75	72	69	68	46	59
	Girls	58	65	56	56	44	54	36
"Teachers who mark examinations too strictly."	Boys	35	41	52	45	42	52	35
	Girls	21	31	37	32	37	43	39
"Getting low marks."	Boys	35	39	41	37	46	54	51
	Girls	29	32	33	28	32	42	29
"Too much homework."	Boys	18	18	32	45	44	58	45
	Girls	4	12	7	29	37	35	36
"Having certain pupils run everything in the school."	Boys	61	46	49	38	37	28	27
	Girls	49	58	56	43	28	42	46

their control of social affairs. But on other items dealing with marks and school work boys are inclined to show more resentment than girls. In general, John's performance on this part of the Inventory was less similar to a typical boy's record than to that typical for girls. He was sufficiently docile, and had sufficient respect for the values exemplified by his teachers, to be fairly "well-adjusted," from his own point of view, to most aspects of the school regime.

5. Comparative Measures of "Adjustment"

The term "adjustment" is ordinarily taken as signifying a smoothly functioning adaptation to some aspect or aspects of an individual's environment. Poor adjustment implies inadequate adaptation, and frequently implies also a degree of associated friction, tension, or emotional disturbance. In practical situations the use of this concept is not without difficulties, for the same behavior that is regarded as maladjusted by one criterion may be an excellent adaptation in terms of some other basis of estimate. Moreover, similar modes of behaving may betoken quite different adjustments in different individuals (or in the same individual at different times); we must, therefore, look with caution upon any attempt to "measure" adjustment and to assign specified values to specified behavior. In the following discussion use will be made of tentative scores based on responses to the Personal-Social Inventory. For each of the three hundred items it has been considered that there is *in general*, a desirable or well-adjusted response, and a less desirable or less well-adjusted response. The reliability and validity of any one item cannot be great, but it is assumed that more often than not the desirable answer accompanies a desirable level of adaptation in a specified category of behavior. As in the case of other types of testing, it is further assumed that reliability and validity can be progressively improved by combining items in a sampling composite.

In individual cases, however, it is only too apparent that scores cannot always be taken at their face value, and that they sometimes show a lack of positive relation, or even a significant inverse relation, to other measures of behavior. In John's case we have an opportunity to examine changes in adjustment scores occurring during critical periods which we already know involved changes in external pressures and in his status in the group.

Figure 18 presents annual standard scores obtained by John in several aspects of self-report, and in a total measure based on eight of these aspects or categories. Looking at these curves in terms of levels and general trends, we note that in items having to do with "School Adjustment" John's self-report places him in a more favorable position than the average for the group, although a downward trend can be noted after the eighth grade. In "Family Adjustment" he showed a distinct downward trend to a position near the maladjusted extreme. In "Social Adjustment" he was consistently below the average, for the most part among the lowest ten per cent of his group.

The unfavorable changes occurring with transition from the sixth grade into junior high school have been discussed in preceding chapters. It is significant, however, that at this time John gave a self-report indicating *improvement* in nearly every category; the only exception is "Family Adjustment," which dropped sharply. In the later years of junior high school, when problems of adjustment became increasingly severe, he began to admit, in many categories, a status similar to that which others assigned to him. In the ninth grade, for example, he appeared extremely maladjusted in the family and social categories, and admitted extreme "Personal Inferiority." Characteristically, he showed little tendency to maladjusted "Over-Statement" or "Assertion of Superiority."

The decline in adjustment scores in the tenth and eleventh grades is perhaps not surprising, but some interpretation is needed to account for the continuation of this

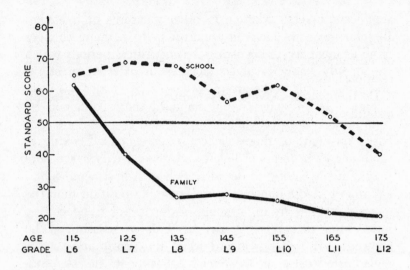

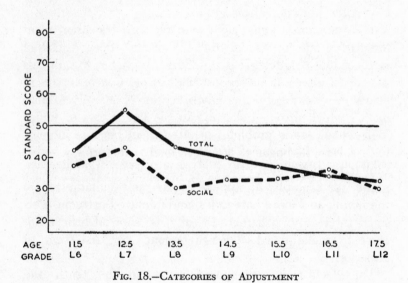

Fig. 18.—Categories of Adjustment

decline into the twelfth grade, when by other criteria (see Chapters III, IV, and V) we know that there were a number of encouraging signs in John's personal status and social relationships.

Do these curves, based on self-report, imply an increasing insight with regard to his basic problems? Do they, perhaps, imply that with actual improvement in status he had become able to face some of these problems more directly and admit their significance?

In reviewing the material reported above, John's counsellor made the following comments, based on an analysis of the Inventory responses without reference to other data: [7]

John's Inventory record presents evidences of an unusually submissive attitude, conflict over submission, dissatisfaction with his family relationships, and an ambivalent attitude toward his parents. Also in evidence are indecision, lack of self-confidence, a feeling of weakness in the face of high aspirations, and an overconcern with various aspects of social recognition. One striking fact is the large discrepancy occurring in each year between the degree of popularity reported by John, and the popularity he wished to attain. In the seventh grade, even though rating himself higher on popularity than in any other year, he admitted being unhappy "some of the time" because "no one liked him." In the eighth grade, a significant change occurred. He assigned to himself very low ratings on all characteristics covered by the Inventory, admitted he was unpopular and did not have nearly as many friends as he wanted. Nevertheless, he denied that he was unhappy over not being liked, denied that he enjoyed a make-believe world, and made no general admissions either as to loneliness or unhappiness. One might expect that a person aware of multiple deficiencies would at the same time indicate some grounds of unhappiness. John's tendency, up to this time, has been to report such feelings only when the conditions he reports do not seem to warrant them. When by his own estimate his status was best, then by his own admission his feelings were gloomiest and he preferred make-believe to reality. An exception to this tendency occurred in the twelfth grade. In this year John's reported feelings corresponded appropriately to other conditions as reported at the same time, thus making it appear that he now had less need to protect himself.

[7] By Judith Chaffey.

The conclusion seems justified that John's responses on this personality schedule are useful in interpreting his development during adolescence. But they cannot be used in a routine manner, or in terms of any fixed specifications as to what adjustment scores "mean." The chief value of the Inventory lies in the possibility of studying significant agreements and disagreements among individual items, and also in the detailed comparison of self-report with information from other sources.

B. JOHN AS A JUDGE OF HIMSELF AND OTHERS

Another, more indirect, form of self-evaluation can be examined in connection with John's judgments on the Reputation Test. In this test, given annually for seven years, it will be recalled that each member of John's class was asked to nominate persons who conformed to certain descriptions as being popular, active, daring, etc. (see p. 35 ff., above). As described in Chapter IV, the judgments recorded on this test were used as an index of a person's status as viewed through the eyes of his classmates. Further analysis has shown that these judgments also offer significant clues as to the characteristics of the judges themselves. In the case of John, it is apparent that his response to the test differs in a number of respects from the reactions typical of his classmates.

1. Association of Traits

On the reputation test certain traits are commonly linked together. One of the more important linkage points is in connection with the trait "popularity." In examining the social values which are implicit in judgments in this test, it is often useful to consider, for any given judge, the characteristics of those persons whom he regards as well liked.

In the case of John, boys whom he thought of as popular he also mentioned, with considerable consistency, as being leaders and as being friendly, active, and happy. The close linkage of these traits is shown by the fact that he attributed the prestige of leadership chiefly to boys whom he regarded as active, and friendly; he also considered that leaders were talkative and had a sense of humor about jokes. With talkative behavior he associated attention-getting, fighting and having a sense of humor. The tendency to be active he associated with friendliness and popularity, and, in the first two years of junior high school, with being restless and assured in class. In these associations he conformed fairly well to group tendencies except in the persistent inclusion of talkativeness, restlessness, and attention-getting in *favorable* trait clusters.

Talkativeness also assumed an important place in John's judgment of girls. It was linked with both leadership and popularity. Being silent he associated with being non-attention-getting, unpopular, and a follower, rather than a leader. This repeated association of talkativeness with both prestige and popularity contributes to the impression that John valued that characteristic quite highly.

It may be noted that for the group as a whole the social significance of talkativeness changed considerably during the course of the study. In the case of boys, the tendency to be silent, not talkative, was a characteristic attributed to popular individuals during the sixth, seventh and eighth grades. Its connotation then turned somewhat neutral, and in the eleventh and twelfth grades "being silent" became a disfavored characteristic. A similar trend was shown by girls, but with an earlier onset and in more clear-cut form; being silent was regarded as a distinct asset among girls in the sixth and seventh grades and being talkative had an unfavorable connotation. At the time of entering high school, unpopular girls began to be described as silent, and by the last year of high school this trait had become a definite handicap; moreover, being outstandingly talkative was now accepted as a socially desirable rather than an undesirable feminine characteristic. It would appear that in his judgments of boys John's guiding values resembled, to some extent, those held by older girls for their feminine classmates.

2. Omission of Items

When a person is troubled about a deficiency in some desirable trait, a common adjustment is to suppress or repress thoughts of that characteristic. This avoidance mechanism may, in the case of the reputation test, lead to the omission of answers on items which awaken unpleasant associations. Although ordinarily thorough and painstaking in his response to tests, on the Reputation Test John omitted more items than the average of his classmates. This tendency to avoid judgments was not shown in the low sixth grade; it increased thereafter and reached a peak in the high ninth and low tenth grade, returning to a normal position in the last year of high school. A rough correspondence can thus be observed between the fluctuations in John's own status in the group, and his readiness to judge the social status of others.

The paired items which he omitted over seventy per cent of the time follow in rank order: Bossy–Submissive; Masculine–Feminine; Daring–Afraid; Social–Unsocial; Enthusiastic–Listless; Absurd–Shy with Adults; Humor about self–Lack of humor about self; Leader–Follower; Fights–Avoids Fights; Good-looking–Not Good-looking; Happy–Sad. As was shown in Chapter IV, these are for the most part traits in which John received a markedly negative unfavorable score in the judgments of his associates.

An interesting trend is revealed in the isolated judgments made by John on some of these items. Girls were the only classmates he ever mentioned as not good-looking, unfriendly, or sad. He never recorded a boy as feminine, but judged two girls as masculine. He mentioned one passive, quiet boy as afraid and lacking in humor, and another as unsocial. He never judged anyone but himself as daring, and this amazing assertion occurred in the year when his reputation in that respect was most negative. Indications such as these suggest the hypothesis that when John was confronted with a description of what he felt to be his own deficiencies he either (1) omitted the item, (2) mentioned himself as having the opposite trait, or (3) projected on girls and occasionally on passive boys, the description of his own deficiency.

3. Conformity with Group Opinion

As an incidental outcome of the reputation test, it is possible to examine the extent to which a person's opinions agree with the social estimates made by the group as a whole. In the adolescent culture, we may assume that a person who "goes along" with the group in his opinion of others will as a rule be more generally favored than a person who has unusual, "queer," evaluations of others. Exceptional conformity may, to be sure, indicate a lack of individual standards. Exceptional disagreement may indicate an unusual degree of maturity or of social perceptiveness. But in many cases disagreement has another possible interpretation, in terms of a bias arising from emotional factors which are known to subjectively color and distort social attitudes.

While still in elementary school, John's opinions concurred fairly well with the majority judgment (73 per cent of complete agreement).[8] In junior high school, however, his views began to diverge from the group, dropping to 43 per cent in the ninth grade. During his first year in senior high school there was almost no agreement (17 per cent) between his judgments and those expressed by the group, but his later records returned to a higher level of conformity.

How shall these trends be interpreted? The increasing divergence, during junior high school, can hardly be attributed to a growth in independent insights, for this was a period when he was often noted as showing a marked degree of social obtuseness; no one would have chosen him, at this time, as a person with an exceptionally penetrating understanding of the social scene. Since John's disagreements with the group were most marked in the years when in general, his group reputation was poorest, we may perhaps infer that his own judgments of social traits were influenced by social status, and by sensitivity to lack of status. When his acceptance by others improved, his social judgments became more objective in the sense that they agreed more closely with the group opinion.

The point could be raised that John was never a "good mixer," and that his non-conformities in opinion might be due in part to an actual lack of knowledge of his classmates. This, however, does not supply a complete explanation of the trends of his judgments. On the whole, he was a better judge of girls (70 per cent) than of boys (57 per cent), although such a difference could hardly be attributed to a

---

[8] For a given trait a judge's conformity with the group was evaluated by scoring his judgment on a scale from 0 to 3, according to whether he mentioned persons who were mentioned rarely or frequently by others. Negative scores were assigned if he mentioned persons who were mentioned by others on the opposite trait. The algebraic average was computed for all traits, and divided by 3 in order to give the percentage of possible "complete" agreement.

better acquaintance with girls. His judgments of friends (57 per cent) was no better than that of boys in general. And his judgment of himself showed only a 10 per cent conformity with group opinion—suggesting that here, in particular, objective appraisal was complicated by factors of a subjective, personal, and emotional origin.

To summarize this analysis of John's responses on the Reputation Test, it has been apparent that during periods of emotional stress he has shown an increased deviation from the characteristics of the group in (1) omission of certain items, and (2) unusual judgments of others. He has also shown a tendency to assign undesirable characteristics to certain of his acquaintances—particularly to his own friends, and to girls. These modes of response, involving mechanisms of avoidance, distortion, and projection, were least in evidence during the sixth and twelfth grades, and most in evidence during the ninth and tenth grades. They serve to indicate not merely the periods of greatest emotional disturbance, but also some of the specific areas of disturbance.

Judging only by the result of this test, the inference may be drawn that during the whole seven-year period, regardless of his current reputation, John was concerned about his lack of rugged masculine virtues—his tendency to be afraid, to be submissive, and to avoid fights. In addition he seems to have been particularly concerned, during the middle period of the study, with his lack of popularity, with his lack of the ability to impress or to lead others, and with his deficiencies in appearance. In formulating his impressions of others, John has also given us a fairly adequate impression of many of his own personal characteristics.

Chapter X

THE STRUGGLE FOR MATURITY

The preceding sections have presented a "montage" rather than a single integrated picture of John's adolescence. Since our interest is in the comparison of techniques as well as in biographical content, the procedure followed has the advantage of presenting side by side a series of special views of development: each taken through its own lens, independent, but corroborative. The limitation of this multiple approach is in part the limitation of science as compared with art. We have denied ourselves the privilege of that intuitive coalescence of the data which would fill in the unknowns and, with broad strokes, present a unified, complete, but somewhat imaginative chronology of an individual career.

In avoiding a single frame of reference, such as is employed, for example, in psychoanalysis, we have at the same time failed to emphasize any single theme in John's development. Stating this in more positive form, we have sought to emphasize a complex plurality of themes. By way of review, however, it may be profitable to bring into clearer relief a number of inter-relationships which seem especially important.

John's adolescence has been described as a period of downs and ups. We have seen evidence of increasing stresses which reached their maximum effect at about the age of fifteen, in the ninth grade. The next three years brought further vicissitudes which were more or less suc-

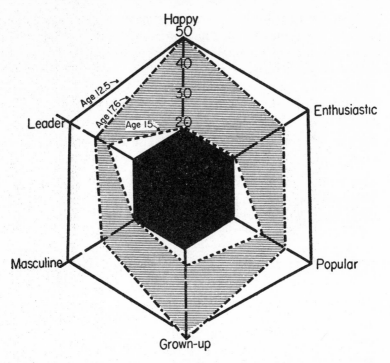

Fig. 19.—Profiles of Reputation Traits

cessfully surmounted; by the senior year of high school John appeared to be definitely on the road toward better personal adjustment and more mature social attitudes.

This can be summarized by comparing representative measures of John's personal and social characteristics at the ages of 12.5, 15, and 17.6, in terms of opinions expressed by his classmates.[1] Figure 19 presents a series of polar coördinate profiles in which standard scores for six reputation traits are plotted on their respective radii. As in previous charts employing standard scores, 20 represents the lower

---

[1] See page 35 ff. for a description of the Reputation Test on which this comparison is based.

end of the distribution, the group mean is at 50, and the S.D. of the group is 10. The outer boundary of Figure 19 indicates some of the more important aspects of John's reputation in these traits at the age of 12.5 years, shortly after his entrance into junior high school. A similar chart, showing only minor differences, could be drawn for John's reputation scores six months and twelve months earlier, when he was still in elementary school. The chief characteristic of this profile is its symmetry and its close approach to an average position in each characteristic. John was very rarely noted by his classmates as either high or low in these traits, and the few unfavorable votes received tended to be balanced by favorable ones. At the age of 15, however, we note a very marked and very general restriction in the trait outline. The reputation scores are squeezed in toward the origin of each axis (that is, toward the lowest possible position in each trait relative to the group).

This shrinking of John's reputation involves a drastic, disheartening change of status in all of the traits represented. In our final record, however, at the age of 17.6, the unfavorable trend has been arrested and on each axis a rebound has occurred toward the average. In two traits ("Happy," "Grown-up") the average has been reached: John is no longer mentioned by his classmates as being unhappy, or as being immature in behavior. In the four other traits some deficiency still remains, but the shaded area provides an indication of the very considerable gains which have taken place.[2] If further evidence is needed as to John's uncertain

---

[2] In two reputation traits, which are not represented above, John's status failed to return toward normal in his later adolescence. In "Active in Games" his standard scores were 43, 35 and 27 in grades 7, 9, and 12 respectively. In "Readiness to Fight" his scores were 44, 20, and 20 for the corresponding grades. These quasi-virile traits are of smaller importance in the more mature culture of seventeen- and eighteen-year-olds than in earlier adolescence. John's continued reputation as being physically passive, and psychologically

but finally more assured progress toward maturity, we can find it in various other aspects of the data. Adult observers agreed that around the age of 15 John was at a low point in, for example, popularity, initiative, and good-naturedness, and at a high point in evidences of anxiety, show-off behavior, and affectation. Their earlier observations (grades 6 and 7) foreshadowed this state of affairs more clearly than did the earlier reputation scores; in fact, the adults' records in the seventh grade provide a better prediction of John's classmate reputation in the ninth grade, than can be found within the classmate records themselves. As for his later career, in all of the traits shown in Figure 19, independent observations by adults have attested to significant gains made by John in his last year of senior high school:

The most outstanding general trend is John's dogged advance toward overcoming his difficulties, particularly in the social sphere.[3]

Mention has been made (Chapter IV) of his friendship with one other boy (Ralph Souza), his emerging humor about himself, his efforts to observe the approved social forms, his increasing ease with classmates and freer conversation with adults.

When we seek a "cause" of the decline and rise in John's personal welfare, we find (as would be expected from any rational theory of personality) that our accounting must include not a single determinant but a complex federation of factors.[4] One factor, however, is so ubiquitous that it insists on special attention. This is the factor of maturity. We have seen in Chapter V that during his junior-high-

---

pacifistic, was therefore less of a handicap in the later than in the earlier grades.

[3] Observational records summary.

[4] For a discussion of the theoretical backgrounds of the present study, see H. E. Jones, "Principles and Methods of the Adolescent Growth Study," *Journal of Consulting Psychology*, Vol. 3, 1939, pp. 157-159.

school years John became markedly shorter, lighter, and punier in relation to classmates. By the age of 15, a turning point had been reached. His rate of growth in height and several other physical dimensions began to be affected by the "adolescent spurt" seen ordinarily among boys a year or so earlier. Changes occurred in primary and secondary sexual characteristics. An increased pulse rate was shown and a sharply increased basal metabolism. These alterations in the physical organism and in its physiological functioning, with their background of profound endocrine changes, could well be expected to have some effect upon behavior —perhaps a greater effect than in a boy who experiences such changes at a more normal age. In the competitive adolescent culture, delayed maturing may lead not only to loss of status with others, but also to the anxiety expressed in the question, "Am I normal?" When the biological innovations of adolescence are at last clearly avowed, a turning point may be reached not merely in physical development, but also in social recognition and in feelings of personal security.

The interpretation followed above stresses the social significance of adolescent changes, and implies that the psychological effect of these changes rests upon the degree to which an individual is sensitive to the norms and values of his social environment. It may be argued, however, that physiological changes can produce psychological effects in a more direct manner. Some of the traits which we tend to associate with "masculinity" are to be noted in a variety of cultures and in many animal species; they are, perhaps, more readily traced to common endocrine factors than to common social factors.

Following this line of thought, to what extent can we regard John's personality patterns and problems of adjustment as a direct correlate of his physical constitution? A parallel has been drawn between "ectomorphy," which is John's dominant physical factor (see p. 74, above) and the so-called behavioral component of "cerebrotonia." This is described by Sheldon et al (*op. cit.*, p. 236) as follows:

The extreme cerebrotonic is an "introvert." He is under strong inhibitory control as regards expression of feeling—he is unable to "let go." His history usually reveals a series of functional complaints: allergies, skin troubles, chronic fatigue, insomnia. He is sensitive to noise and distractions. He is not at home in social gatherings and he shrinks from crowds. He meets his troubles by seeking solitude.

Such a description fits John in many respects but errs in some. Usually unable to "let go" emotionally, he sometimes expresses himself vigorously and persistently. He is not at home in social gatherings, but nevertheless often presses upon the social group instead of meeting his troubles by complete withdrawal. It is, however, not surprising to find disharmonies and inconsistencies in John's psychological as well as physical development. The life history of an individual involves variations on basic themes, some part of which, at least, are determined by his biological make-up.

From still another point of view, it may quite properly be urged that these physical and physiological factors would have exerted a very different impact upon a child developing under different environmental conditions. Shall we not assign a rôle to the economic factor, which as we have seen was a burdensome problem to his family during most of John's school life? Its effect was manifested in countless ways—in family dietetics planned to meet a skimpy budget rather than to satisfy the needs of a growing organism; in clothing, which in John's case was not far from the neighborhood standard, but which provided little margin for comfort or display (with occasional renewals of sweater and slacks, John did not climb to the status of owning a suit until he reached the ninth grade). Even greater were the effects of economic pressure upon John's use of leisure. Movies and other recreation were rationed. Few were the opportunities to do things and visit places which would widen his contacts with the community life about him, and many were the requirements of home chores and household routines.

This brings us to an even more basic environmental factor: John's relation to his mother, his reaction to her overprotective attitudes, and to her self-centered demands for service and attention. The importance of this aspect of John's life history would justify a more detailed discussion than circumstances permit us to present. Earlier sections, however, have suggested some of the problems arising from this family situation, and some hints at least have been given as to the nature of John's dependence upon his mother. As a little boy the cords by which his mother bound him were both a comfort and a source of resentment; his first hesitant tugging at these apron strings was later followed by more or less vehement rebellion. It will be recalled that John's own report showed indications of exceptional increases in family strain during the adolescent period. It would be true to say that he was a problem to his mother, but a more primary fact is that his mother was a problem to him. This does not imply, however, that we are seeking to place upon her any special burden of censure; such information as we have suggests that with the time and the motive we could readily demonstrate a very relevant earlier chain of ante-cedents in her own childhood, and in her relationships to John's grandparents. Unrecognized by John, the hand that rocked (or failed to rock) his mother's cradle, reached across the years to intervene in a thousand situations in-volving John himself.

There were other ways in which physical make-up played an important rôle in his complex patterns of adjustment. We have seen that late maturing, in his case, was superimposed upon an earlier record of illness and physical weakness; in physical abilities he was different from his classmates not merely because of immaturity, but also because of deep-seated, possibly constitutional deficiencies in physique. Even when the processes of maturing eventually brought some relief, we have been aware of limitations imposed by a lack of harmonious growth in various parts of the body; the normal balance and timing of development were by no means fully realized.

It cannot be doubted that John's deficiencies in physical ability, most evident in the ninth grade, reacted unfavorably upon his position in the group and upon his own adjustment. For the boys in this sample, the relationship has been studied between popularity and physical ability, strength, intelligence, achievement, home rating (socio-economic status), and height.[5] At the eight- and ninth-grade levels, the only individual factors correlating significantly with popularity were those based on physical ability and strength. Evidence was found that

... among adolescents, the premium placed upon dexterity in games is high. It is correspondingly demonstrated that what adolescents of low physical ability lack in that trait must be made up in clear superiority in other traits ... such areas of compensation as friendliness or enthusiasm, cheerful attitude, humor, and assurance have been shown to serve.

John, however, was handicapped not only by his lack of athletic prowess and associated abilities, but also by personal traits which emphasized rather than compensated for his other deficiencies. We have noted in earlier sections that his unskillfulness in activities enjoyed by other boys marked

---

[5] P. Bower, *The Relation of Physical, Mental and Personality Factors to Popularity in Adolescent Boys.* Ph.D. Dissertation, University of California, 1941.

him as "queer"; it made for social isolation, and his response to this lowered status was to develop characteristics which further increased his unpopularity. John's delayed maturity was clearly one of the important elements in this web of relationships, but it must be thought of as accentuating rather than as solely producing the basic problems which he faced in social adjustment. Even with a normal timing of maturational processes, John would still have been relatively weak in traits which are usually prized by boys during the early teens.

In later adolescence these deficiencies became of smaller importance, partly because of changing social values and partly also because of a process of maturing that is expressed in social structures as well as in organisms. The naïve like-mindedness characteristic of a younger group broadens, at a later age, into a greater variety of special interests. Special sympathies and appreciations in this more differentiated society give the individual a greater range of choice—a greater opportunity to select his own appropriate environment.

John's improved adjustment in the twelfth grade (and later, in college)[6] was to some extent owing to the fact that he was at last able to find a congenial social rôle, among others who appreciated his special qualities and who made demands that were not impossible to meet. Thus, the more favorable situation and prognosis for John, as he reached the end of senior high school, were due partly to changes in John as he laboriously caught up with the group, but we must give credit also to changes in the group as they caught up with John, and as their values and standards of achieve-

---

[6] In his freshman year at college John was rated by his college advisor as somewhat quiet, shy, and unexpressive, but was given markedly favorable ratings in other areas: as having a quick comprehension and strong, well-developed intellectual interests; as being unaffected, independent, and showing initiative; and as having "a pleasing personality."

ment came closer to the sober aspirations which John had always held important.

As was noted in the introduction, the study of single cases is likely to yield conjectures and hypotheses rather than general conclusions. At least one conclusion, however, can be lifted out of the developmental history presented here. It is, perhaps, a little like the conclusion to be drawn from a Horatio Alger story. John Sanders was a boy with an extraordinary accumulation of personal handicaps: physical, social, emotional, economic. He was unsupported by any special sense of security in his family; unaided by any special gift of intelligence or by any special insights on his part or on the part of his teachers. He reached a low point in adjustment, but he did not remain there. The greater personal stability and the more adequate social relationships he achieved in the last year of high school were carried forward during college. His college years also brought a successful record in courses and in an enterprising variety of outside activities. So marked an upturn in John's personal fortunes is evidence not only of the toughness of the human organism but also of the slow, complex ways in which nature and culture may come into adaptation.

INDEX